## The Accused

Jeffrey Archer's latest play, *The Accused*, is a tense courtroom drama with a difference. The audience will act as the jury, as if they were in the Central Criminal Court at the Old Bailey.

You will have to decide . . .
 Did Dr Sherwood murder his wife?
 Was Jennifer Mitchell his mistress?
 Which of his alibis should you believe?

The choice will keep you on the edge of your seats, and at the end of the trial you will be invited to deliver your verdict of guilty or not guilty. Once you have made that decision, the play will continue – with one of two different endings, depending on your verdict. Only then will you finally discover the truth.

**Jeffrey Archer** is one of Britain's top-selling novelists. He is published in 63 countries and 32 languages, and has international sales passing one hundred and twenty million copies. He is a former Member of Parliament and Deputy Chairman of the Conservative Party, and was created a Life Peer in the Queen's Birthday Honours of 1992. He is also an amateur auctioneer, conducting some 60 charity auctions each year.

He has written ten novels, several of which have been serialised for television and radio, four sets of short stories, and three plays. His first – *Beyond Reasonable Doubt*, starring Frank Finlay and Wendy Craig, ran at the Queen's Theatre, in London's West End, for over 600 performances. His second play, *Exclusive*, which ran at the Strand Theatre, starred Paul Scofield, Eileen Atkins and Alec McCowen.

Jeffrey Archer is now working on his eleventh novel, *Serendipity*, which will be published in May 2002.

# The Accused

*by*

## Jeffrey Archer

**Methuen Drama**

Published by Methuen Drama

1 3 5 7 9 10 8 6 4 2

First published in 2000 by Methuen Publishing Limited

Copyright © 2000 Jeffrey Archer

Jeffrey Archer has asserted his rights under the Copyright, Designs and
Patents Act, 1988, to be identified as the author of this work

ISBN 0 413 76840 6

Typeset by SX Composing DTP, Rayleigh, Essex

# The Accused

*The Accused* was presented by Lee Menzies at the Theatre Royal, Haymarket, London, on 5 December 2000, having received its world premiere performance at the Theatre Royal, Windsor, on 26 September 2000.

The cast was as follows (in order of appearance)

| | |
|---|---|
| **Jury Baliff** | Edward de Souza |
| **Anthony Kersley QC** | Michael Feast |
| **Alison Ashton** | Janet Wantling |
| **Sir James Barrington QC** | Edward Petherbridge |
| **Andrew Jarvis** | Dominic Kemp |
| **Court Usher** | Neil France |
| **Mr Justice Cartwright** | Tony Britton |
| **Patrick Sherwood** | Jeffrey Archer |
| **Guard** | Richard Hodder |
| **Detective Chief Inspector Payne** | Douglas Fielding |
| **Albert Webster** | David Weston |
| **Masood Hussein** | Madhav Sharma |
| **Professor Alistair Forsyth** | David Collings |
| **Jennifer Mitchell** | Emma Davies |
| **Foreman of the Jury** | The voice of Ken Livingstone |
| **Second Guard** | Gary Taylor |

All the action takes place in Court Number One at the Old Bailey.

Time: the present day.

| | |
|---|---|
| *Director* | Val May |
| *Designer* | Simon Higlett |
| *Lighting Designer* | Vince Herbert |
| *Sound Designer* | Frank Bradley |
| *Company Stage Manager* | Debbie Cronshaw |
| *Deputy Stage Manager* | Jane Allen |
| *Assistant Stage Managers* | Angharad Watson, Rebecca Kilgariff, Nathalie Hobday |

# Act One

## Scene One

*The Jury Room, Central Criminal Court, the Old Bailey. Morning.*

*When the audience take their seats, there is no curtain. The stage is dark, but at the front is a door marked JURY ROOM. On the wall is a clock showing 9.45 a.m. When the house lights go down, the door opens and the* **Jury Bailiff** *steps through it and addresses the audience.*

**Jury Bailiff**  Good morning Ladies and Gentlemen of the jury. Welcome to the Old Bailey. My name is Gilbert Pierce and I have been appointed your jury bailiff. You have been summoned this day to appear at the Central Criminal Court. The trial you have been selected for is the Crown versus Mr Patrick Sherwood. Mr Sherwood is charged with murder. In a few moments I will take you through to Court Number One. But as I suspect this is the first time you've been called on to give jury service, you may well have some questions, and as this is my one hundred and fourteenth murder, I may just have some of the answers.

Now the judge in this case is Mr Justice Cartwright who considers himself to be the natural successor to Judge Jeffreys and his views on the restoration of the death penalty are well documented. However, you will be relieved to learn that he's considerate with jurors, but uncompromising when it comes to barristers – especially those who try to take advantage of him. And while I'm on the subject of barristers, both the Crown and the Defence in this case are represented by two of the best – and they both know it.

Sir James Barrington leads for the Defence, while Mr Anthony Kersley, a former Member of Parliament, appears for the Crown. If you sense any friction between them, don't be surprised: they loathe each other. It's no secret that Sir James defeated Mr Kersley by one vote to become Chairman of the Bar Council, and was awarded the knighthood that goes with it. It's also common knowledge that they haven't exchanged a civil word since.

*The spotlight falls on* **Kersley** *and his junior,* **Ashton**, *who are moving towards the courtroom in a corridor of light.*

**Ashton**    I see we're up against your old sparring partner.

**Kersley**    Are you referring to Barrington, or His Lordship Mr Justice Cartwright?

**Ashton**    I thought you and Sir James . . .

**Kersley**    Frankly I've never cared for either of them, and I can assure you the feeling is mutual. You see, I didn't go to the right school, old boy.

*The attention moves to* **Barrington** *and* **Jarvis**.

**Jarvis**    Have you appeared before Mr Justice Cartwright before?

**Barrington**    Many times, and on this occasion we start with a home advantage.

**Jarvis**    Why's that?

**Barrington**    Because he disapproves of Kersley almost as much as I do, so all we have to do is massage the old boy's ego.

**Jarvis**    But surely Kersley will do exactly the same thing?

**Barrington**    Not a chance. He'll pick a quarrel with Cartwright at the first possible opportunity – he believes in the old adage that a good row with the judge makes up for a weak case.

**Jury Bailiff** *looks up from his clipboard.*

**Jury Bailiff**    Once Mr Kersley has made his opening statement for the Crown, he will proceed to call his witnesses. At the moment there are five on the list, but I'm not expecting to get through all of them today. After the adjournment you may return home, when you will quickly discover that friends and relatives will want to discuss your views on the case and will be only too willing to offer theirs. But unlike you, they will not have heard all the evidence, so their opinions are, at best, worthless and, at worst, injurious. The safest bet is don't talk to anyone and don't allow anyone to talk to you

**Usher**   Mr Pierce, I am instructed by His Lordship to ask if the jury are assembled and ready?

**Jury Bailiff**   They are all in attendance, Mr Usher.

**Usher**   Then will you please accompany the jury to the courtroom?

**Jury Bailiff** *(bows, and the Usher returns the bow.* **Jury Bailiff** *turns back to face the audience)*   Ladies and Gentlemen of the Jury, please follow me.

**Kersley** *and* **Ashton** *walk through the jury door towards the courtroom in a corridor of light.*

**Ashton**   Do you think in the twenty-first century anyone gives a damn which school you went to?

**Kersley**   Mr Justice Cartwright doesn't belong in the twenty-first century – as you're about to find out – which may even work to our advantage.

**Ashton**   What do you mean?

**Kersley**   Simply that if the jury considers the judge is favouring one side, they quite often react against it.

**Ashton**   I can't believe he'll make it that obvious.

**Kersley**   Then I'll have to make sure he does.

**Barrington** *and* **Jarvis** *follow in the corridor of light.*

**Barrington**   Andrew, have you had a chance to speak to our client this morning?

**Jarvis**   Yes, when I left him he was pacing up and down his cell and feeling rather sorry for himself. (*Pauses.*) I have to admit I rather like him.

**Barrington**   After thirty years in this game Andrew, I can tell you that murderers are a far nicer class of person – it's the barristers you have to watch out for.

**Jarvis** (*laughs*)   Are you referring to Mr Kersley, by any chance?

**Barrington**   I never refer to Kersley if I can avoid it. However, don't lower your guard even for a moment, because when it comes to punching, no one has explained to Kersley where the belt is.

*As* **Barrington** *enters the courtroom, the two QCs come face to face for the first time. They give each other a cursory nod. A few moments later there is a triple knock on the outside of the door.*

**Usher**   Be upstanding in the court. All persons having anything to do before my Lords, the Queen's Justices, oyer and terminer, and general gaol delivery for the jurisdiction of the Central Criminal Court, draw near and give your attendance. God save the Queen.

**Mr Justice Cartwright** *enters and takes his place in the centre of the bench. All bow. The* **Judge** *returns their bow.*

**Usher**   Bring up the prisoner.

**Sherwood** *steps into the dock, and the Jury Bailiff walks across to stand in front of him.*

**Jury Bailiff**   Is your name Patrick Hugh Sherwood?

**Sherwood**   Yes.

**Jury Bailiff**   Patrick Sherwood, you stand charged with murder. The particulars of the offence are that, on the twenty-first of March 1999 in the county of London, you administered a fatal dose of poison to your wife, Elizabeth Sherwood. How say you – Guilty or Not Guilty?

**Sherwood**    Not guilty.

**Jury Bailiff** (*walks to the front of the stage, faces the audience and bows*)    Members of the Jury, the defendant stands before you charged with one count – that of murder. To this count he has pleaded Not Guilty. By his plea he has cast himself upon his country, which country ye are. Your charge, therefore, is to hearken unto the evidence and say whether he be guilty or no. (*He turns his attention away from the audience and returns to his place.*)

**Judge**    Members of the Jury, you have sworn to try this case on the evidence. You must therefore give heed only to what takes place in this court and ignore anything you have read in the press. Mr Kersley, you may proceed with the prosecution.

**Kersley**    May it please Your Lordship, Members of the Jury. The murder of Elizabeth Sherwood was a crime planned by a man with a brilliant and subtle mind, who set out to dupe his colleagues, so that when his wife died, no one would suspect him of being involved in such an evil enterprise.

But unfortunately for him, even the cleverest of murderers make mistakes which, like pieces in a jigsaw, end up revealing the true picture.

The Crown will produce five pieces of that jigsaw, which will show the lengths to which Mr Sherwood was willing to go in order to cover his tracks. Once those five pieces are in place, I believe you will come to one conclusion: that Mr Patrick Sherwood is guilty of murder.

My Lord, we call our first witness, Chief Inspector Payne.

**Usher**    Call Chief Inspector Payne.

**Guard**    Chief Inspector Payne.

*The* **Usher** *stands and announces* **Chief Inspector Payne**, *as he will do for all other witnesses from the lobby outside the double doors. He then shuts the door and returns to his seat. The* **Chief**

**Inspector** *enters and takes his place in the witness box. Whenever witnesses speak, they should face the jury – the audience.*

**Usher** Take the testament in your right hand and read from the card.

**Payne** I swear by Almighty God that the evidence I shall give shall be the truth, the whole truth and nothing but the truth.

**Kersley** Is your name Alan Payne and are you a Detective Chief Inspector with the Central Area major incident team?

**Payne** Yes, I am, sir.

**Kersley** Chief Inspector, can you tell the court how you became involved in this case.

**Payne** (*Checks his notebook and faces the* **Judge**.) May I refer to my notebook, My Lord?

**Judge** (*nods*) You may, Chief Inspector.

**Payne** On the evening of March the twenty-first 1999 we received an emergency call at Wimbledon police station, from a Mr Albert Webster, the porter of a block of flats in the division. He informed us that he thought a burglary had taken place and, as there had been several in the area recently, we immediately went round to Arcadia Mansions to investigate.

**Kersley** And what did you find when you arrived at the Sherwoods' flat?

**Payne** I found Mrs Sherwood lying on the floor, covered in a blanket. She was sobbing and holding up her right arm, which appeared to be badly bruised. I assumed that she must have taken an intruder by surprise, but when I asked her what had happened she was incoherent. She kept pointing to a glass of wine on a side table. A few moments later an ambulance crew arrived and after they had examined her, told me that she must be taken into hospital immediately.

**Kersley**    Did you follow the ambulance to St George's?

**Payne**    No, my first priority was to take a statement from the porter before checking over the flat.

**Kersley**    And once you had done that, were you still of the opinion that a burglary had taken place?

**Payne**    No, I was puzzled. There was clearly evidence of a struggle, but I could find no sign of a forced entry. All the locks and windows were intact, with the exception of a kitchen window, which led on to the fire escape and was slightly open. No drawers appeared to have been left open, which is what one would expect if a burglary had taken place.

**Kersley**    Did anything else arouse your suspicions?

**Payne**    A rubber glove that had been dropped on the kitchen floor, and I was also curious about the glass of wine Mrs Sherwood had been pointing to, so I instructed forensics to have the glove and the wineglass sent to the lab for testing.

**Kersley**    Did you then go to the hospital?

**Payne**    Yes, as I hoped Mrs Sherwood might have recovered sufficiently to answer some questions.

**Kersley**    And was she able to do so?

**Payne**    No, she died a few minutes after I arrived at St George's.

**Kersley**    And the cause of death, Chief Inspector? How was it entered on the death certificate?

**Payne**    Congestive cardiac failure, but as Mrs Sherwood had suffered in the past from (*Checks his notebook.*) atherosclerosis, her heart attack was not considered to be suspicious.

**Barrington**    My Lord, I apologise for interrupting, I simply wish to seek your guidance.

**Judge** (*suspiciously*)   Yes, I'm listening, Sir James.

**Barrington**   Is the Chief Inspector a qualified medical practitioner? Because if he isn't, perhaps we could dispense with his medical opinions and stick to the facts in this case.

**Judge**   You were not seeking my guidance, Sir James, but simply wishing to make a point. No doubt you feel you have. Carry on, Mr Kersley.

**Kersley**   Thank you, My Lord. Chief Inspector, you were telling the court, before we were interrupted by my learned friend, that you went to the hospital in the hope of asking Mrs Sherwood some questions. When you arrived, did you find Mrs Sherwood in her husband's arms?

**Judge** (**Barrington** *rises*)   Mr Kersley, that was an outrageous leading question whose only purpose was to prejudice the jury.

**Kersley**   I do apologise, My Lord. I must have been distracted by Sir James's unnecessary interruption. Chief Inspector, when you arrived at the hospital, was Mr Sherwood at his wife's bedside?

**Payne**   No, sir, a member of the hospital staff was trying to locate him.

**Kersley**   I see. So who signed the death certificate?

**Payne**   Her local GP, a Dr Haslam.

**Kersley**   And was he satisfied that Mrs Sherwood had suffered a heart attack?

**Payne**   He had no reason to believe otherwise. He'd been treating her for a heart condition for some time.

**Barrington**   My Lord, he is at it again.

**Judge**   And so are you, Sir James. Carry on, Mr Kersley.

**Kersley**   Did you also accept this judgement?

**Payne**    I saw no reason to question their professional opinion.

**Kersley**    So what caused you to change your mind and open a murder inquiry?

**Payne**    Some weeks later I received a call from the dangerous drugs division of the Home Office. Following that call, I visited a chemist in Wellingborough to check their Controlled Drugs Register. It showed that a Mr Sherwood had been regularly having prescriptions of Potassium Chloride made up, that fell into the category of poisons under the 1994 Drug Trafficking Act.

**Kersley**    Why should that make you consider a crime had been committed? After all, Mr Sherwood has the authority to write out such prescriptions.

**Payne**    Yes, but why have them made up outside London when St George's Hospital has a large pharmacy of its own?

**Kersley**    Why indeed, and did Mr Sherwood collect these prescriptions himself?

**Payne**    No, over a period of three months he used a Ms Jennifer Mitchell, a junior staff nurse at St George's, to collect them on a Saturday in Wellingborough and then return the ampoules of Potassium to Mr Sherwood's office on the Monday morning.

**Kersley**    Chief Inspector, would I be correct in saying that if Ms Mitchell had not volunteered a statement, you would never have considered charging the defendant?

**Payne**    That is correct. Her evidence was to prove vital. She stated that over a period of twelve weeks, between January and March of 1999, Mr Sherwood had instructed her on six occasions to pick up ten-millilitre ampoules of Potassium Chloride. But he only handed her the prescriptions on a Friday evening, when he knew she would be visiting her parents in Wellingborough.

**Judge**   Wellingborough keeps cropping up, Chief Inspector. Does it have some particular significance in this case?

**Kersley**   Wellingborough has no relevance in itself, My Lord. All Mr Sherwood needed was for the prescriptions to be dispensed at a chemist outside London, so that none of his colleagues at St George's would be aware of what he was really up to.

**Judge**   Ah, so it could well have been Milton Keynes or Henley?

**Kersley**   Yes, My Lord, but only if Ms Mitchell had lived in Milton Keynes or Henley.

**Judge**   Ah, yes, I see. Carry on, Mr Kersley.

**Kersley**   Chief Inspector, were any of these prescriptions for Potassium Chloride made out for Mrs Sherwood?

**Payne**   No, they were all prescribed for his private patients.

**Kersley**   So what made you think that they might not have reached those patients?

**Payne**   When the results of the lab test came back, they showed that there were traces of Potassium Chloride on the rubber glove found on the Sherwoods' kitchen floor.

**Kersley**   On the glove, I see . . . and did the lab tests reveal anything else of significance?

**Payne**   Yes, the glass of wine found on the table by Mrs Sherwood's side contained thirty millilitres of Temazepam, which is three times the recommended dosage.

**Kersley**   And did you identify any fingerprints on that glass?

**Payne**   Yes, Mrs Sherwood's.

**Kersley**   But did you also check the fingerprints on the wine bottle?

**Payne**   Yes, I did, and we could only find Mr Sherwood's.

**Kersley**   Only Mr Sherwood's. But what about the rest of the flat?

**Payne**   The only other fingerprints identifiable were those of the porter, Albert Webster.

**Kersley**   So there was no reason to believe there had ever been an intruder?

**Payne**   None that we could discover, sir.

**Kersley**   Once you had gathered all your evidence, what did you do next?

**Payne**   I obtained a warrant for the arrest of Patrick Sherwood, which I executed on June the ninth at St George's Hospital. I cautioned him, and then charged him with the murder of his wife, Elizabeth Sherwood.

**Kersley**   Thank you, Chief Inspector. No more questions, My Lord.

**Judge**   Sir James, do you wish to cross-examine the Chief Inspector?

**Barrington**   I most certainly do, My Lord. Chief Inspector, I must begin by asking you if it is usual to open a full murder inquiry on information supplied by one young woman.

**Payne**   No, but . . .

**Barrington**   No buts, Chief Inspector, it was a simple enough question and the answer was no. My next question is equally simple. The bruises on Mrs Sherwood's arm. Surely the most likely explanation is that they resulted from a struggle with an intruder? You told us there had been several burglaries in the area recently.

**Payne**   I could find no evidence of a burglary, sir.

**Barrington**   Chief Inspector, is it common for burglars to leave their fingerprints all over the place, hoping you will find them?

**Payne**   No, but . . .

**Barrington**   I thought we'd agreed on no buts, Chief Inspector. Can I also confirm that it was you who discovered the kitchen window open?

**Payne**   Someone had unlatched it from the inside.

**Barrington**   It hardly matters who unlatched it, Chief Inspector, only who might have used it as a means of entry, and I do hope you're not going to suggest that Mr Sherwood entered his own flat by the fire escape, when he could so easily have walked in through the front door.

**Payne**   Unless he had a reason for not wanting to be seen walking in through the front door.

**Barrington**   And on that flimsy supposition you decided to charge Mr Sherwood with murder?

**Payne**   No, that decision was made by the Crown Prosecution Service after they had considered all the evidence.

**Barrington**   I see. So let me finally ask you, Chief Inspector, when you charged Mr Sherwood, did he make any statement?

**Payne**   Yes. (*Checks his notebook.*) He said, 'This is ridiculous. I adored my wife; someone must have been feeding you with false information'.

**Barrington**   Someone must have been feeding you with false information. Now, I wonder who that can have been? No further questions, My Lord. (*He resumes his seat.*)

**Judge**   Do you wish to re-examine, Mr Kersley?

**Kersley** (*rises slightly*)   No, thank you, My Lord.

**Judge**   Thank you, Chief Inspector. You may leave the witness box. (*The* **Chief Inspector** *leaves the witness box and the courtroom.*) Perhaps you'd like to call your next witness, Mr Kersley.

**Kersley**   Yes, My Lord. I call Mr Albert Webster.

**Usher**   Call Mr Albert Webster.

**Guard**   Mr Albert Webster.

**Webster** *is a man aged between forty-five and fifty. He is wearing a T-shirt and a well-worn suit. He enters the courtroom, looking lost, and the* **Usher** *has to guide him to the witness box.*

**Usher**   This way, sir. Please take the testament in you right hand and read from the card.

**Webster**   I never bothered with the reading.

**Usher**   Then repeat after me, I swear by Almighty God.

**Webster**   I swears by Almigh'y God.

**Usher**   That the evidence I shall give.

**Webster**   That the evidence I shall give.

**Usher**   Shall be the truth, the whole truth and nothing but the truth.

**Webster**   Shall be the truth, the 'ole truth and nothin' but the truth. (*He stares at the* **Judge**.)

**Judge**   Mr Webster, there's no need to address your remarks to me. It is the jury who will want to hear all your evidence.

**Kersley**   Is your name Albert Philip Webster?

**Webster**   You got it, mate.

**Kersley**   And where do you live?

**Webster**   Arcadia Mansions, Arcadia Road, Wimbledon.

**Kersley**   And what is your occupation?

**Webster**   I'm the resident porter – 'ave been for the past twelve years, 'aven't I, ever since I came out of the army.

**Kersley**   Mr Webster, can you tell the court why the late evening of March twenty-first 1999 is etched on your memory?

**Webster**   I dunno if it's etched on me memory, but I won't never forge' it.

**Kersley**   So please tell the court what happened that night, Mr Webster.

**Webster**   It must 'ave been around 'alf past ten, 'cos that's when I goes on me night round 'fore turnin' in. Always starts at the top of the building and works down to the bottom, where I live. It's only logic, innit? When I reached the landin' of the sixth that night, I 'eard noises comin' from the floor below.

**Kersley**   Can you describe those noises?

**Webster**   Yes, it was as if someone was 'avin a row, and then I 'eard a crash – like a chair turnin' over.

**Kersley**   A row? Could it have been a quarrel between a man and his wife?

**Barrington** (*rises*)   My Lord, how can Mr Webster possibly know the answer to that question?

**Webster**   Cos I 'eard voices.

**Judge**   Voices? Can you be certain, Mr Webster, that you heard more than one voice coming from the flat?

**Webster**   No, I can't be certain, but why would Mrs Sherwood want to shout at 'erself?

**Kersley**   Why indeed. And did you hear anything she said?

**Webster**   Yes, I'm pretty sure I 'eard 'er say ''ow did you get in?'.

**Kersley**   'How did you get in.' And did she sound surprised?

**Webster**   Too bloody right she did.

**Judge**   Moderate your language in my court, Mr Webster.

**Webster**   Sorry, Guv.

**Judge**   You address me as My Lord, and counsel as Sir.

**Webster** (*looking directly at the* **Judge**)   Right you are, sir. (*He turns his attention back to* **Kersley**.)

**Kersley**   Had you been inside Mrs Sherwood's flat before?

**Webster**   Oh, yes, when I gets to 'er floor, she'd often ask me in for a cup'a tea, I think she liked the company.

**Kersley**   But wasn't Mr Sherwood around most evenings?

**Webster**   No, not regular. In any case, I wouldn't 'ave gone in if he was around, not after that time he came back unexpected and told me to bugger off. (**Judge** *and* **Webster** *look at each other.*)

**Kersley**   And how often did Mr Sherwood go out in the evenings?

**Webster**   Quite a lot. What with his private patients and so on.

**Kersley**   How did you know that he was going out to see one of his private patients?

**Webster**   I used to watch 'im leavin' from my flat in the basement, didn't I.

**Kersley**   Yes, I'm sure you did, but that doesn't explain how you knew that he was visiting a patient?

**Webster**   Common sense, inn't (*He touches his nose.*) Whenever he was visitin' a patient, he'd take his doctor's bag with him, wouldn't he.

**Kersley**    And was he carrying his doctor's bag that night?

**Webster**    No, he wasn't.

**Kersley**    What time was it when he left the building?

**Webster**    It must 'ave bin a few minutes after seven.

**Kersley**    How can you be so sure?

**Webster**    Cos I'd just come out of the lavatory, 'adn't I. (**Kersley** *looks puzzled*.) I phones me ol' mum at six, tea at 'alf past, go to the toilet at seven, *Coronation Street* at seven thirty – regular as clockwork. Old army training, innit.

**Kersley**    And when did Mr Sherwood return that night?

**Webster**    No idea, Guv, but it can't 'ave been before eleven could it, cos he wasn't there when they carted his wife off to 'ospital.

**Kersley**    Quite. So when you heard the row, what did you do next?

**Webster**    I ran down the stairs, fast as I could. I bangs on the door, but no one answers.

**Kersley**    Was that when you called the police?

**Webster**    No, Guv, I decided this 'ad to be one of them emergencies, where I'm expected to use me master key. In the Pioneer Corps it's what we used to call initiative.

**Webster** *holds up a bunch of keys, showing one in particular, and waits while everyone hangs on his words.*

**Kersley**    But you told the judge that before you unlocked the door, you had heard more than one voice coming from the flat?

**Webster**    Yes, I'm pretty (*He hesitates*.) sure about that.

**Kersley**    Could one of those voices have been Mr Sherwood's?

**Webster**   Doesn't seem likely on account of the fact that
he'd already gone out.

**Kersley**    But could he have returned without you seeing
him?

**Webster**   Only if he used the fire escape.

**Kersley**    Well, that would certainly explain Mrs
Sherwood's words, 'How did you get in?' So, Mr Webster,
when you unlocked the door, what did you find?

**Webster**   Some furniture had been knocked over and Mrs
Sherwood was lyin' on the floor moanin'.

**Kersley**    And was she on her own?

**Webster**   Yes, as far as I could tell.

**Judge**    What do you mean, Mr Webster, by 'as far as I
could tell'?

**Webster**   Cos the door on the far side of the room
slammed shut the minute I walked in, didn't it. (**Judge**
*makes a note.*)

**Kersley**    Slammed shut the minute you walked in – as if
someone had hurriedly pulled it closed?

**Webster**   Yes, you got the idea.

**Kersley**    So what did you do next? (**Barrington** *nods.*)

**Webster**   I dials 999 and tells 'em to send round an
ambulance an' the police sharpish, an' then I gets a blanket
and covers 'er up.

**Kersley**    Did she give any reason why the furniture had
been knocked over?

**Webster**   No, she was just lying there, moanin' and
rubbin' 'er arm what was bruised, so I offered 'er the glass of
wine that was on the table 'opin it would 'elp, but she just
pushed it away, and then she began cryin' even louder. So I

wondered if someone 'ad put somethin' in the wine that had made her ill.

**Barrington** (*rises*)    My Lord . . .

**Judge**    Yes, yes, Sir James. (*Faces the audience.*) Members of the Jury, you should ignore that comment – it is nothing more than speculation. Carry on, Mr Kersley.

**Kersley**    No more questions, My Lord. I think the jury has taken the point.

**Webster** *starts to leave the witness box.*

**Judge**    Mr Webster, please remain in the box for a moment, as I have a feeling that Sir James might want to ask you a question or two.

**Barrington**    You are quite right, My Lord. Mr Webster, may I begin by congratulating you on your remarkable memory.

**Webster**    Thank you, Guv. I s'pose you can put it down to my army trainin'.

**Barrington**    Quite so, but even I was puzzled, Mr Webster, as to how you could be so sure that when Mr Sherwood left the building, on the night in question, he was not carrying his doctor's bag. (**Kersley** *smiles.*)

**Webster**    To be honest, Guv, I wasn't sure at the time.

**Barrington**    You weren't sure at the time, but you stated categorically . . .

**Webster**    No, I wasn't categoric, not until I phoned for the ambulance.

**Barrington**    Not until you phoned for the ambulance. I'm not altogether certain I'm following you, Mr Webster.

**Webster**    Well, you see, that's when I first saw the doctor's bag. He'd left it on the table by the phone, so he couldn't 'ave taken it wiv 'im, could he?

**Barrington**   I see. Mr Webster you told the court that you thought someone else might have been in the room when you first unlocked the door to the apartment.

**Webster**   Yeah, I did.

**Barrington**   And your immediate reaction when you saw the overturned furniture was that it must have been a burglar whom Mrs Sherwood had been shouting at?

**Webster**   Yes, cos there 'ave been a lot of break-ins durin' the past year, aven't there?

**Barrington**   Have there? Now, Mr Webster, remembering what a good memory you have, is it possible you can tell the court when you heard the sentence 'How did you get in?'. Was it before you unlocked the door, as you opened the door, or after you had entered the room?

**Webster**   Before I unlocked the door.

**Barrington**   So, some time before you stepped into the room?

**Webster** (*hesitates*)   Yes, I think so.

**Barrington**   When you walked in, you told my learned friend that you saw the door on the far side of the room slam shut?

**Webster**   Yeah, I did.

**Barrington**   Could it have been the wind?

**Webster**   I s'pose so.

**Barrington**   Did you check to see if anyone was hiding in the kitchen?

**Webster**   No. Why should I?

**Barrington**   Because it leads to the kitchen window and fire escape.

**Kersley**   My Lord, I am enthralled by Sir James's gift for storytelling and indeed I would go as far as to suggest that were he to submit this particular scenario to the BBC they might well consider it for *A Book at Bedtime*. But I'm bound to ask what it has to do with the case now being tried before Your Lordship?

**Barrington**   It goes to the very heart of this case, My Lord, because the Prosecution are claiming that the defendant poisoned his wife, when there is no evidence to show that he was even in the building when she collapsed. It now seems there is a distinct possibility that someone else was and therefore the police could well have arrested the wrong person.

**Judge**   Ingenious, Sir James. But I do feel the jury might require a little more proof of the existence of your phantom intruder.

**Barrington**   You may even see them in the witness box, My Lord . . .

**Kersley** (*leaps up*)   Is Sir James suggesting that it was Mr Webster who murdered Mrs Sherwood?

**Webster**   Are you accusin' me?

**Barrington**   If Mr Kersley had allowed me to finish my sentence, I would have added 'before this trial is over'. No further questions, My Lord.

**Webster**   I did hear her say ''ow did you get in?''.

**Judge**   Do you wish to re-examine, Mr Kersley?

**Kersley**   No, thank you, My Lord.

**Webster**   I wasn't tellin' no porkies.

**Judge**   You may leave the box now, Mr Webster.

**Webster**   And I *did* see the door slam. (*Remains in the witness box.*)

**Judge**   Mr Webster, will you please leave the courtroom. (**Webster** *reluctantly leaves.*)

**Webster**    On my mother's life, I swear I saw it slam shut!
(*He walks off, aided by* **Guard**.)

**Guard**    This way, sir.

**Webster**    I only told 'em what you told me to say!

*The lights fade on all members of the court as* **Webster** *exits.*
*Blackout as sound of bells is heard.*


## Scene Two

*Later that afternoon.*

*When the lights come up* **Mr Hussein** *is in the witness box. He is*
*between forty and fifty, formally dressed, and speaks with a pronounced*
*Indian accent. The Koran should be wrapped in a cloth.*

**Usher**    How will you take the oath, Mr Hussein.

**Hussein**    On the Koran, sir.

**Usher**    Take the Koran in your right hand and read from
the card.

**Hussein**    I swear by Almighty Allah that the evidence I
shall give shall be the truth, the whole truth and nothing but
the truth.

**Kersley**    Your name is Masood Hussein, and you are the
proprietor of Hussein the Chemist, 141 High Street,
Wellingborough?

**Hussein**    Yes, sir I am.

**Kersley**    Mr Hussein, perhaps you could tell the court
how you became involved in this case.

**Hussein**    I read in one of the medical journals of the
premature death of Mrs Elizabeth Sherwood. I wouldn't
have given the matter a second thought, had it not been for
an accompanying photograph of the mourners attending the
funeral.

**Kersley**   Why were the mourners of any significance, Mr Hussein?

**Hussein**   I observed a lady standing a few paces behind Mr Sherwood whom I thought I recognised. I studied her face more closely with a magnifying glass and realised I had seen her before, but couldn't remember where.

**Kersley**   And did you eventually remember?

**Hussein**   Yes, it was some days later when I was making an entry in my register of poisons and came across the signature of a Ms J. Mitchell at the top of the page, and recalled that she had visited the pharmacy several times.

**Kersley**   Can you be certain that it was the same Ms Mitchell whose photograph you saw?

**Hussein**   Oh, yes, I checked back through the register and discovered that Ms Mitchell had called in to the pharmacy on six separate occasions during a period of three months, and always on a Saturday.

**Kersley**   But that doesn't prove she was the woman in the photograph?

**Hussein**   But Mr Sherwood's signature does.

**Kersley**   Mr Sherwood's signature?

**Hussein**   Yes, he had countersigned all the prescriptions.

**Kersley**   Had he? And what were these prescriptions made out for?

**Hussein**   Ten millilitres of Potassium Chloride.

**Kersley**   And did you keep all six prescriptions?

**Hussein**   I most certainly did, Mr Kersley. I retain all prescriptions for controlled drugs for the required period of five years.

**Kersley**  You say you served Ms Mitchell on no fewer than six occasions. Do you recall anything in particular about her?

**Hussein**  She was a self-confident young woman and although she knew exactly what she wanted, she appeared tense, even a little nervous.

**Kersley**  And is that what made you suspicious?

**Hussein**  No, I was more puzzled than suspicious, because I couldn't work out why Mr Sherwood would want to have his prescriptions made up in my small pharmacy in Wellingborough, when St George's has a large pharmacy of its own. From my experience, doctors want drugs immediately, not some days later.

**Kersley**  Mr Hussein, an ampoule of Potassium Chloride was found in Mr Sherwood's bag on the night of his wife's death. Could it have came from your shop?

**Judge**  How can Mr Hussein know the answer to that question?

**Hussein** (*turning to face the* **Judge**)  My Lord, if I could see the ampoule I would be able to tell if it had come from my shop.

**Judge**  How is that possible, Mr Hussein?

**Hussein**  Because every dangerous drug has a number displayed on its packaging which, when it is sold, has to be entered in my poisons register.

**Kersley**  My Lord, both the poisons register and the ampoule of Potassium found in Mr Sherwood's bag are in the court's possession. They are numbers eleven and twenty-six on the court's list of exhibits. Perhaps Your Lordship would be kind enough to check the entry in the register, while I ask Mr Hussein to read out the number on the ampoule of Potassium. (**Judge** *nods his agreement.*)

**Barrington**    My Lord, I must object. This parlour game adds nothing to the evidence. After all, the ampoule of Potassium found in Mr Sherwood's bag was unopened so what possible bearing can it have on the case?

**Judge**    A great deal Sir James, because if this is not one of the ampoules collected from Wellingborough, it will surely work in favour of your client, as it will show that there is no proof that the other five ever left the hospital. (**Jury Bailiff** *hands the register up to the Bench, while the* **Usher** *hands over the ampoule of Potassium to* **Hussein**.) Please read out the number on your package, Mr Hussein.

**Hussein**    107293 AZ.

**Judge** (*nods, and faces the audience*)    They are identical.

**Kersley**    So there can be no doubt that the ampoule of Potassium picked up by Ms Mitchell on March the nineteenth from Mr Hussein's shop, was the one found in the defendant's bag on the night of Mrs Sherwood's death, and therefore we can assume that the other five . . .

**Barrington**    My Lord, that is outrageous. We can assume nothing . . .

**Kerlsey**    Other than that my learned friend will always interrupt whenever he finds his client in any real trouble. No more questions, My Lord. (*Resumes his seat.*)

**Judge**    Do you wish to question this witness, Sir James?

**Barrington**    I most certainly do, My Lord. Mr Hussein, do you keep a box of dusting powder and a brush under your shop counter?

**Hussein** (*puzzled*)    No, sir, I do not.

**Barrington**    What about a fingerprint pad?

**Hussein**    A fingerprint pad?

**Barrington**    A pair of handcuffs, perhaps?

**Hussein**    Why should I do that?

**Barrington**   Because you seem to enjoy playing the amateur detective.

**Hussein**   I'm not sure I know what you mean, Sir James.

**Barrington**   Then allow me to explain. You come across a photograph of Mr Sherwood in a medical journal attending his wife's funeral. With the help of a magnifying glass you spot a lady in the crowd whom you think you recognise. You discover her name in your drugs register and suddenly you're the Sherlock Holmes of Wellingborough.

**Hussein** (*looks puzzled*)   I don't know a Mr Holmes.

**Barrington**   You don't?

**Hussein**   I don't recall him ever coming into the shop.

**Barrington**   When did you arrive in this country, Mr Hussein?

**Hussein**   Just over two years ago.

**Barrington**   Only two years ago, so you're probably still unfamiliar with our ways, not to mention our literature?

**Hussein**   I have long been an admirer of the British, Sir James.

**Barrington**   I feel sure you have, Mr Hussein, but that doesn't make you British. Did you qualify in this country?

**Hussein**   No, sir, I did not.

**Barrington**   Then why are you allowed to dispense dangerous drugs?

**Hussein**   Because I have been a member of the Royal Pharmaceutical Society for the past twenty years.

**Barrington**   On what grounds, may I ask?

**Hussein**   Because in my own country I am a qualified doctor.

**Barrington**    But you are not in your own country, Mr Hussein, so I must ask you, do your qualifications permit you to practise, as a doctor, in this country?

**Hussein**    No, sir, but . . . that is purely . . .

**Barrington**    No buts, Mr Hussein. They do not permit you to practise as a doctor in this country!

**Hussein**    Sadly, not yet.

**Barrington**    Or perhaps not so sadly, for the patients.

**Kersley**    My Lord, is my learned friend going to be allowed continually to insult the witness in this manner?

**Judge**    Mr Kersley, this is a charge of murder and, within the bounds of reason, I shall allow the Defence every latitude.

**Kersley**    Is that latitude to be extended to Sir James asking questions to which he already knows the answer?

**Judge**    Only a foolish lawyer asks questions to which he does not know the answer, Mr Kersley. Please carry on, Sir James.

**Barrington**    Thank you, My Lord. Mr Hussein, have you ever visited St George's Hospital?

**Hussein**    No, sir, though I have . . .

**Barrington**    Have you ever come into contact with Mr Sherwood?

**Hussein**    Yes, I attended a lecture he gave to the King's Fund.

**Barrington**    Along with how many other people, may I ask?

**Hussein**    There must have been over a hundred people present.

**Barrington**    I doubt if even Mr Sherlock Holmes would have gleaned enough evidence from going to a lecture, attended by over a hundred people, to conclude that the lecturer should be charged with murdering his wife. If that were sufficient evidence, you'd be claiming we're old friends simply on the strength of this cross-examination.

**Hussein**   I wouldn't dream of doing so, Sir James, especially as we have met before.

**Barrington**   And when, pray, was that?

**Hussein**   It was just over a year ago, when you were chairman of the Bar Council and addressed the Anglo-Indian Society – of which I have the honour of being Secretary.

**Barrington**   And how many people were present on *that* occasion.

**Hussein**   Just over three hundred.

**Barrington**   Just over three hundred.

**Hussein**   Yes, but we did sit next to each other during dinner. At the time you left the Society in no doubt that you felt most Indians ran corner shops and you thought it amusing that you were still unable to tell one from another. However, I would not ask Sir Arthur Conan Doyle to consider that as evidence of anything.

**Barrington**   I'm delighted that we've finally found something we can agree on, Mr Hussein, because convicting Mr Sherwood will depend on substantiated evidence, and not on the arm's-length opinion of an unqualified chemist. No further questions, My Lord.

**Judge**   Do you wish to re-examine, Mr Kersley?

**Kersley**   Yes, thank you My Lord. I do have one question for Dr Hussein . . . I beg your pardon, My Lord . . . Mr Hussein, may I ask you why you were so willing to assist the police in their enquiries, even agreeing to appear in this case as a Crown witness?

**Hussein**   To do one's duty as a good citizen and respect the law is the British way, Mr Kersley. Or that's what Sir James assured us when he delivered his lecture to the Anglo-Indian Society last year.

**Kersley**   No more questions, My Lord.

**Judge**   Thank you Mr Hussein, you may leave the witness box. (**Hussein** *leaves the witness box and passes in front of* **Kersley**.).

**Kersley** (*aside to* **Hussein**)   Dr Hussein, you're wasted on the medical profession – you should have joined us at the Bar.

**Hussein**   Oh, no, Mr Kersley, I'm far too honest to make a success of your chosen profession.

**Judge**   You may call your next witness, Mr Kersley.

**Kersley**   Thank you, My Lord. I call Professor Alistair Forsyth.

**Usher**   Call Alistair Forsyth.

**Guard**   Alistair Forsyth.

**Professor Forsyth** *is a Scot of around fifty-five to sixty, very formal and slightly pompous. He enters the courtroom and goes straight to the witness box. He takes the card in his right hand, as if he has been through the process many times before. He does not wait for the* **Usher** *to instruct him.*

**Forsyth**   I swear by Almighty God that the evidence I shall give shall be the truth, the whole truth and nothing but the truth.

**Kersley**   Professor, I would like to establish with the jury the particular expertise you bring to this case. (**Forsyth** *nods.*) You were educated at Edinburgh Academy, from where you won a scholarship to Cambridge to read medicine?

**Forsyth**   Yes, Mr Kersley, that is correct.

**Kersley**    At Cambridge you graduated with honours in Pharmacology and went on to do research for an MD?

**Forsyth**    That is also correct.

**Kersley**    On completing your MD, you took up a Fellowship at King's College, London, where you continued your research. May I enquire what your specialist subject was?

**Forsyth**    Toxicology, the study of poisons.

**Kersley**    You were offered the Chair of Toxicology at London University, and you have since written several books on the subject, which are acknowledged as the recognised text for any student reading for a medical degree?

**Forsyth**    Only three of my works are set texts, Mr Kersley. The rest of them would be far beyond the understanding of the average undergraduate.

**Kersley**    Quite so. You are a Fellow of the Royal Society and have recently been awarded a CBE for services to medicine?

**Judge**    I do believe, Mr Kersley, that you have established beyond peradventure the credentials of your expert witness, so perhaps the time has come to get on with the case in hand.

**Kersley**    I am delighted to learn, My Lord, that you feel Professor Forsyth's credentials need no further claims on my part, as I believe your endorsement can only give the jury added confidence in his opinions.

**Judge** (*scowls*)    Mr Kersley. Get on with it.

**Kersley**    First let me ask you, Professor, how you became involved in this case?

**Forsyth**    The Crown Prosecution Service invited me to make a report on Mrs Sherwood's medical history. I began by reading all Mrs Sherwood's files held at St George's.

**Kersley**    And would I be correct in thinking that you sought a Home Office order to exhume the body?

**Forsyth**    I would have done so, Mr Kersley, had Mr Sherwood not given instructions for the body to be cremated a few days after her death.

**Kersley**    Really. Despite this setback, were you able to discover any new evidence?

**Forsyth**    No, because Mr Sherwood had misled his colleagues into believing that his wife's previous heart attack explained her premature death. They also emphasised that as she was married to a surgeon who specialised in the subject, her aftercare treatment could hardly have been better.

**Kersley**    Or worse, as the case may be.

**Judge**    Mr Kersley, you will in future desist from making these *sotto voce* remarks. (*Turns to the audience.*) Members of the Jury, Mr Kersley's comment should be ignored.

**Kersley**    But not forgotten, I suspect.

**Judge**    Did you wish to say something, Mr Kerlsey?

**Kersley**    My Lord, I was simply at pains to point out that . . .

**Judge**    It is not your responsibility to point out anything, Mr Kersley, merely to ask questions, which may elicit answers that in turn might possibly assist the jury.

**Kersley**    But . . . My Lord . . . if I am to discharge . . .

**Judge**    No buts, Mr Kersley, as Sir James has so properly reminded us. From you, I only require questions. I expect the answers to come from the witnesses.

**Kersley**    So be it, My Lord. Professor, would it be possible for an experienced doctor to poison a patient while at the same time fooling his colleagues?

**Forsyth**   Yes, nowadays that would be easy enough for anyone with Mr Sherwood's experience. There are three known poisons -- only one available on prescription - that would kill an intended victim without leaving any clue that a murder had taken place.

**Kersley**   Well, I will deal only with the one poison that is available on prescription - Potassium Chloride. Professor, could you poison someone with Potassium Chloride and hope to get away with it?

**Forsyth**   Oh, yes, it's the most satisfactory of all poisons for a would-be murderer. Once injected, the victim will suffer a cardiac arrest, showing absolutely no sign of being poisoned.

**Kersley**   So what led you to suspect that this was not a death by natural causes?

**Forsyth**   The discovery of a deposit of Potassium Chloride on the rubber glove found on the floor of the Sherwoods' kitchen.

**Kersley**   And how much poison was discovered on the glove?

**Forsyth**   One milligram, which is an amount consistent with checking that a hypodermic needle was working effectively.

**Kersley**   Would you care to demonstrate to the jury exactly what you mean by that, Professor?

**Forsyth**   Certainly. (*Pulls on a rubber glove and demonstrates to the audience.*) Just before injecting a patient, you press the plunger thus, to ensure that the liquid is flowing. (*He allows it to fly into the air, landing on his glove.*) As you observe, some droplets end up on the glove.

**Kersley**   And this led you to believe that Mrs Sherwood had probably received an injection of Potassium Chloride just before her death?

**Forsyth**   Yes, it did.

**Kersley**   And could such an injection also have caused the bruising on her arm?

**Forsyth**   Most certainly it could, especially if she had offered any resistance.

**Kersley**   Professor, I should now like to ask you about the glass of wine found on the table by Mrs Sherwood's side. Have you been able to analyse its contents?

**Forsyth**   Yes I have, and they revealed large deposits of Temazepam – a particularly strong sedative, available only on prescription. There was enough left in the glass to have knocked out a heavyweight boxer.

**Kersley**   Which would, had she taken it, have made injecting her all the more easy.

**Barrington**   My Lord, I was accused by my learned friend of a plot worthy of *A Book at Bedtime*. Following Mr Kersley's flight of fancy, once this trial is over can I assume he will be applying to become an investigative journalist with the *News of the World*?

**Judge**   We will leave the jury to decide which one they consider the better qualified for that job, Sir James. Carry on, please, Mr Kersley.

**Kersley**   Professor, can you confirm that six ampoules of Potassium Chloride were collected by Ms Mitchell from a chemist in Wellingborough?

**Forsyth**   Yes, I can. I studied the poison register and checked all six entries against the prescriptions collected by Miss Mitchell and they all tallied.

**Kersley**   And as a leading authority on the subject, would you now tell the court how many ampoules of Potassium Chloride it would take to cause a fatal heart attack?

**Forsyth** (*hesitates*)    Four ampoules would be certain to cause cardiac arrest, but a fifth would leave no hope of survival.

**Kersley**    And how would the victim die, Professor?

**Forsyth**    In great pain, before the heart finally gave out.

**Kersley**    But surely the post-mortem would reveal strong traces of Potassium Chloride that would cause the examining doctor to become suspicious?

**Forsyth**    Unfortunately not. A heart attack causes an unusual amount of Potassium to be released into the bloodstream, which would be regarded as quite normal by any doctor conducting a post-mortem.

**Kersley**    And Mr Sherwood would have been aware of this?

**Forsyth**    A first-year medical student would have been aware of it.

**Kersley**    Professor, what would be your opinion of a doctor who took advantage of such specialised knowledge?

**Forsyth**    It betrays the very principles of the Hippocratic Oath, 'Whatever house I enter, there will I go for the benefit of the sick, refraining from all wrong doing.' The meaning could not be clearer.

**Kersley**    No more questions, My Lord.

**Judge**    Sir James. Do you wish to cross-examine?

**Barrington**    Thank you, My Lord. Dr Forsyth.

**Forsyth**    Professor.

**Barrington**    I do apologise, Professor. May I begin by congratulating you on such an illustrious career, detailed so laboriously by my learned friend. But do you consider, as a scientist, you are also qualified to pass moral judgements on a colleague without relying on a shred of evidence?

**Forsyth** The Hippocratic Oath is the very foundation of a doctor's code of practice.

**Barrington** And there is nothing in Mr Sherwood's equally distinguished career to suggest that he doesn't agree with you. So let us now consider the facts, Professor. You told the court that none of the doctors at St George's gave you any reason to believe that Mrs Sherwood had died in unusual circumstances.

**Forsyth** That is correct, but none of them was aware that Mr Sherwood had been collecting ampoules of Potassium Chloride from a chemist outside London.

**Barrington** I will come to that, Professor. Now, in your long report commissioned by the Crown Prosecution Service, you also confirm (*Holds up the report.*) that Mrs Sherwood's GP had her on the correct programme of medication for the particular heart problem she was suffering from?

**Forsyth** Yes, but Dr Haslam was not . . .

**Barrington** I wonder, Professor, if you would be kind enough to confine yourself to answering my questions and not making speeches. This courtroom is not an extension of your lecture theatre and I am not one of your undergraduates. So allow me to move on to the constituents of Potassium Chloride and, may I say, Professor, how much we all enjoyed your little demonstration with the hypodermic needle, which you claimed was consistent with the amount of the chemical found on the kitchen glove.

**Forsyth** (*now angry*) It most certainly was.

**Barrington** But tell me, Professor, as an acknowledged expert on the subject, would it not also be consistent with the amount of Potassium found in this bottle of grapefruit juice, which is more likely to be located in a kitchen?

**Forsyth** Yes, but . . .

**Barrington**    Search as I might, I couldn't find any reference to grapefruit juice in your hundred-and-thirty-nine-page report.

**Forsyth**    My report was not concerned with . . . the contents . . .

**Barrington**    Then perhaps it should have been. Professor, you told the court that the first thing you did when you were asked to look into this case was to study Mrs Sherwood's medical history.

**Forsyth**    And I did so.

**Barrington**    And so did I, Professor, and I discovered that Mrs Sherwood's father had died of a heart attack at the age of fifty-eight. Why didn't you consider this possible hereditary condition worthy of mention?

**Forsyth**    Because I could find no connection between the death of a thirty-seven-year old woman and her father's demise at fifty-eight. Had you been one of my undergraduates Sir James, you would have learnt that research is one thing, being able to draw scientific conclusions from it is quite another.

**Barrington**    Well, let us consider some of your scientific conclusions, shall we, Professor, and try to find out what you have learnt from them. On how many occasions have you testified for the crown in murder trials where poisoning was involved?

**Forsyth**    A dozen – more, perhaps.

**Barrington**    And was one of those cases 'The Crown versus Mr Roger Latham'?

**Forsyth** (*embarrassed*)    Yes, it was.

**Barrington**    And were you called by the prosecuting counsel as an expert witness?

**Forsyth**    Yes, I was.

**Barrington**    And was it your evidence that influenced the jury to return a verdict of guilty?

**Kersley** (*leaps up*)    My Lord, is my learned friend questioning Professor Forsyth's integrity?

**Judge**    Are you, Sir James?

**Barrington**    Certainly not. But I would refer your Lordship to the Judge's summing up, and I quote, (*He picks up a book and quotes from the trial.*) 'I find the evidence presented by Professor Forsyth as compelling, and feel it should weigh heavily with the jury when they come to consider their verdict.'

**Judge**    In the judge's summing up. I see. Please continue, Sir James.

**Barrington**    Did you tell the court on that occasion that after you had carried out extensive laboratory tests, you were in no doubt that the liquid Mr Roger Latham poured into his brother's coffee not only poisoned him, but was responsible for his premature death?

**Forsyth**    That was my opinion at the time.

**Barrington**    At the time. I see. And did another professor later prove that when the liquid was poured into hot coffee it was immediately neutralised and couldn't have poisoned a mouse?

**Forsyth**    Yes, but there was no way of knowing that then. It was some years later . . .

**Barrington**    I was not suggesting, even for one moment, Professor, that you were culpable, only human, like the rest of us and therefore capable of making mistakes. Remind me, what verdict did the jury reach on that occasion?

**Forsyth**    Guilty.

**Barrington**    And did Mr Latham die in gaol, having served fourteen years of his life sentence?

**Forsyth** (*nods*)   Yes, I believe he did.

**Barrington**   And, two years after his death, did his family receive an unconditional pardon from the Home Secretary?

**Forsyth** (*softly*)   Yes, but the antitoxic properties of that particular substance were not discovered until . . .

**Barrington**   Until it was too late, Professor. But fortunately it is not too late in this case. Professor, you have already confirmed that the amount of Potassium Chloride found in Mrs Sherwood's bloodstream was consistent with a heart attack.

**Forsyth**   What I actually said was . . . .

**Barrington**   Yes or no, Professor? It either was consistent with a heart attack or it wasn't.

**Forsyth** (*hesitates*)   Yes, it was.

**Barrington**   Could someone with Mrs Sherwood's medical history have suffered a heart attack, if she had been surprised by an intruder? Yes or no?

**Forsyth**   Yes, it's possible.

**Barrington**   And are you aware of any other doctors who have prescriptions made up outside of the hospital they work in? Yes or no?

**Forsyth**   Yes.

**Barrington**   And could the amount of Potassium Chloride found on the rubber glove have been concentrated grapefruit juice? Yes or no?

**Forsyth**   Yes, I suppose it could.

**Barrington**   And if Potassium Chloride is taken in small doses, isn't it harmless – and in certain cases even beneficial? Yes or no?

**Forsyth**   Yes, but . . .

**Barrington**    Shall we dispense with all these buts, Professor, and remove any doubt in the jury's mind once and for all? I wonder, My Lord, if I might be shown exhibit twenty-six, the ampoule of Potassium Chloride that was found in Mr Sherwood's bag, which Mr Hussein identified as coming from his shop.

**Judge**    For what purpose, Sir James?

**Barrington**    Like the distinguished professor, My Lord, I wish to conduct an experiment.

**Judge**    I do hope you're not wasting the court's time, Sir James.

**Barrington**    Heaven forbid, My Lord. I simply wish to prove my client's innocence.

*The* **Judge** *nods to the* **Usher** *who removes the ampoule from* **Sherwood**'s *bag and hands it over to* **Barrington**, *who breaks the ampoule and drinks it slowly.*

**Barrington**    A little dry for my taste, but as you can see, Professor, not fatal. So let us hope that once again it will not be your expert evidence who allows an innocent man to rot in gaol for the rest of his life.

**Kersley**    My Lord, this goes far beyond the bounds of . . . legitimate cross-examination . . .

**Judge**    You are quite right, Mr Kersley. Sir James, that comment was unforgivable, and I must insist that you withdraw it immediately.

**Barrington** (*pauses*)    My Lord, I am unable to do so.

**Judge**    And why is that, Sir James?

**Barrington**    I was the defence counsel in The Crown versus Mr Roger Latham and I will go to my grave aware that my feeble advocacy failed to save the life of an innocent man. I am determined that it will not happen a second time. No further questions, My Lord.

*The lights slowly dim and everyone's eyes remain on* **Barrington**.
*The curtain falls, but goes back up during the interval, to reveal the jury
door back in place.*

CURTAIN

# Act Two

### Scene One

*The following morning.*
*The stage remains dark, but the audience can still see the jury room door. On the wall, the clock is showing 9.45 a.m. When the house lights dim, the* **Jury Bailiff** *steps through the door and addresses the audience.*

**Jury Bailiff**   Good Morning, Ladies and Gentlemen of the Jury and thank you for reporting back in good time. The second day of the trial will begin with Mr Kersley's final witness, Ms Jennifer Mitchell. Ms Mitchell is the Crown's principal witness, so I would not be surprised if she was in the witness box for most of the day.

Please continue to be vigilant when it comes to discussing this case with anyone not on the jury. If there are no questions, we should make our way back to Court Number One. Ladies and Gentlemen of the Jury, please follow me.

*The* **Jury Bailiff** *steps through the door, and when the lights come up, we are back in Court Number One, where we discover the barristers are talking among themselves while they await the entrance of the* **Judge** *and jury.*

**Ashton**   I've just bumped into Ms Mitchell as she was coming up the steps.

**Kersley**   What's she wearing?

**Ashton**   Smartly tailored blue suit, very conservative, and virtually no make-up.

**Kersley**   Good, that's exactly the image I want fixed in the jury's mind.

**Ashton**   And I reminded her to refer to her father, Councillor Mitchell, as often as possible.

**Kersley**   And under no circumstances to mention the reason she left St George's at such short notice?

**Ashton**    It was the last thing I emphasised.

**Kersley**    Good. Then we can only hope that Sir James doesn't know the real reason.

*The attention moves across to* **Barrington** *and his junior,* **Jarvis**.

**Barrington**    And so we finally come up against their star witness.

**Jarvis**    And how do we feel about that?

**Barrington**    If Ms Mitchell is as innocent as Mr Kersley would have us believe, we're in a lot of trouble.

**Jarvis**    Surely not, after the roasting you gave Webster and Forsyth yesterday.

**Barrington**    Yes, but try not to forget the doctor's bag. Kersley made me feel like a pupil who'd just arrived in chambers, so if under his guidance Ms Mitchell proves a little too convincing, I may have to take the odd risk.

**Jarvis**    What do you have in mind?

**Barrington**    I might even consider asking the occasional question to which I do not know the answer. So if I put out my hand, (*He makes a gesture.*) make sure you pass me a blank sheet of paper.

**Usher**    Be upstanding in the court. All persons having anything to do before my Lords, the Queen's Justices, draw near and give your attendance. God save the Queen.

*All rise as* **Mr Justice Cartwright** *enters and resumes his place. All bow and he returns the bow.*

**Usher**    Bring up the prisoner. (**Sherwood** *enters the dock.*)

**Judge** (*to the audience*)    Ladies and Gentlemen of the Jury, good morning. Mr Kersley, you may call your next witness.

**Kersley**    Thank you, My Lord. I call Jennifer Mitchell.

**Usher**    Call Jennifer Mitchell. (*A woman of thirty, attractive and dressed in smart suit, enters the witness box.*)

**Guard**   Jennifer Mitchell.

**Usher**   Take the testament in your right hand and read from the card.

**Mitchell** (*quietly*)   I swear by Almighty God that the evidence I shall give shall be the truth, the whole truth and nothing but the truth.

**Kersley**   Is your name Jennifer Alice Mitchell and are you presently working as a senior staff nurse at Wellingborough Cottage Hospital?

**Mitchell**   Yes, I am.

**Kersley**   Did you previously work at St George's Hospital, Tooting?

**Mitchell**   Yes, I did.

**Kersley**   And was the consultant in charge of the cardiac unit the defendant, Mr Patrick Sherwood?

**Mitchell** (*avoids looking at the dock*)   Yes, he was.

**Judge**   Can you please speak up, Ms Mitchell. The jury (*He waves a hand, sweeping the audience.*) will need to hear every word you have to say. (**Mitchell** *nods.*)

**Kersley**   When you first began working for Mr Sherwood, what were your responsibilities?

**Mitchell**   I was a junior staff nurse attached to the cardiac unit.

**Kersley**   And did Mr Sherwood ever ask you to carry out any duties not directly related to your work on the cardiac unit?

**Mitchell**   Yes, a few months after I'd started working at St George's, Mr Sherwood asked me to pick up a sedative for his wife from the hospital pharmacy, which I was happy to do.

**Kersley**    Understandably. You would want to please your boss.

**Judge**    Mr Kersley, that was both leading as well as an opinion. Do not further try my patience.

**Kersley** (*facing the judge*)    I will attempt very hard not to do so, My Lord. (*Turning back to* **Mitchell**.) Ms Mitchell, did Mr Sherwood ask you to collect any other prescriptions from the hospital pharmacy?

**Mitchell**    Yes, but that would be quite normal practice for any of the nurses.

**Kersley**    But then one Friday evening he asked you to pick up a prescription from outside London?

**Mitchell**    Yes, that was just before I was leaving to spend the weekend with my parents in Wellingborough and he instructed me *not* to have that prescription made up at the hospital pharmacy.

**Sherwood**    I did no such thing – I've never asked you to pick up any of my prescriptions in Wellingborough.

**Mitchell**    But you did tell me *not* to have them made up at St George's.

**Sherwood**    I most certainly did not . . .

**Judge**    Mr Sherwood, you must not interrupt the witness while she is being questioned by counsel, now sit down (**Sherwood** *reluctantly sits down.*). Carry on, Mr Kersley.

**Kersley**    Thank you, My Lord. Did Mr Sherwood give any explanation as to why you shouldn't have the prescription made up at the hospital pharmacy?

**Mitchell**    No, he just said that it was for a private patient.

**Kersley**    Is that also normal practice?

**Mitchell**    No, I had never been asked to do that before by any doctor.

**Kersley**    Did you question Mr Sherwood about this?

**Mitchell**    No one questioned Mr Sherwood about anything – not even Sister.

**Kersley**    And was this prescription also for a sedative?

**Mitchell**    No, it was for ten millilitres of Potassium Chloride.

**Kersley**    Did he ever ask you to pick up any more ampoules of Potassium Chloride?

**Mitchell**    Yes, he did. It must have been about two weeks later – also on a Friday evening, and he asked me to drop it back to his office on Monday morning.

**Kersley**    And how many times did he ask you to have prescriptions for poison made up outside London?

**Mitchell**    Half a dozen times during the next three months.

**Kersley**    I apologise, Ms Mitchell, but I must now ask you an embarrassing question as I want the jury to understand fully why you became so willing to fall in with Mr Sherwood's plans. During the time leading up to Mr Sherwood asking you to collect these prescriptions from Wellingborough, did he maintain a professional relationship with you?

**Mitchell**    To begin with he did, but then he started to give me presents, send me flowers and even invited me out to dinner.

**Kersley**    And did you accept any of these invitations?

**Mitchell**    No, not immediately, but then he became more and more insistent, and it's quite difficult for a junior nurse to go on refusing the senior consultant. So I finally gave in and agreed to have dinner with him at a restaurant in Fulham, where he assured me no one would recognise us.

**Kersley**    So he chose the restaurant, but did you make the booking?

**Mitchell**    No, he did. And he paid for the meal in cash –
he explained that way it couldn't be traced back to him.

**Kersley**    And did he invite you out again?

**Mitchell**    Oh, yes. After that, Patrick regularly invited me
out for a meal, or to the theatre. He kept telling me how
lonely he was. And then one night on the way home, he said
he was falling in love with me.

**Kersley**    What was your reaction?

**Mitchell**    I was very flattered at the time, and when we
arrived back at my flat he asked if he could come up for
coffee.

**Kersley**    And did you agree to his request?

**Mitchell**    No, I made some excuse about having to be up
early for morning rounds. I didn't mind having dinner with
him, but I wasn't willing to begin a relationship with a
married man, especially one who was working at the same
hospital.

**Kersley**    Quite understandably. But that later changed?

**Mitchell**    Yes, it was a few weeks later, at the staff
Christmas party – he pulled me under the mistletoe and
started kissing me.

**Kersley**    But isn't that normal at a Christmas party, Ms
Mitchell?

**Mitchell**    Yes, but it isn't normal for a doctor to put a
hand on your breast.

**Kersley**    And how did you respond?

**Mitchell**    I pushed him away and then left the party as
quickly as possible, hoping that none of the other nurses had
noticed.

**Kersley**    And did you go straight home?

**Mitchell**    I would have done so, but he followed me out. He apologised immediately and asked if he could walk me back to my flat.

**Kersley**    Did you let him?

**Mitchell**    Yes, I lived less than a mile away and he seemed very contrite.

**Kersley**    And did he leave you once you arrived back at your flat, Ms Mitchell?

**Mitchell**    No, he asked if he could come in for coffee.

**Kersley**    And did you agree this time?

**Mitchell**    Yes, I'm afraid I did. You see, on the way home he never stopped telling me how much he adored me and longed to be with me. And in any case, it had started to rain and I felt rather sorry for him.

**Kersley**    So after he'd joined you in the flat, what happened next?

**Mitchell**    I made us some coffee, but he hung around long after he'd drunk it. I pointed out that it had stopped raining, but he just wouldn't go.

**Kersley**    And did he once again try to kiss you?

**Mitchell**    Yes, he did.

**Kersley**    Forgive me for being indelicate, Ms Mitchell, but how far did it go?

**Mitchell** (*looks at the* **Judge**)    Do I have to answer that question, My Lord?

**Judge**    Yes, indeed you do, Ms Mitchell. You see the jury need to know exactly what took place that night.

**Mitchell** (*hesitates*)    We ended up making love.

**Sherwood**    We've never made love and you know it.

**Judge**    Mr Sherwood, I have already spoken to you about interrupting this witness.

**Sherwood**    My Lord, do I have to sit in silence while this woman goes on telling lies about me?

**Judge**    You must listen to all the witnesses without interrupting, Mr Sherwood. You will in time be given an opportunity to answer questions from the witness box under oath, if you choose so to do. But until then, you will remain silent. (**Sherwood** *sits down.*) Carry on, Mr Kersley.

**Kersley**    So, after Mr Sherwood had made love to you, did he eventually leave?

**Mitchell**    Yes, it must have been about three in the morning.

**Kersley**    And how did he treat you the following day?

**Mitchell**    He was very courteous and professional during ward rounds, but that changed when he asked me to join him in his office.

**Kersley**    Why, what happened, Ms Mitchell?

**Mitchell**    As soon as I walked in, he pulled me towards him and started to undo my uniform. I warned him that anyone might come in.

**Kersley**    What did he say to that?

**Mitchell**    He didn't, he just smiled and locked the door.

**Kersley**    And did he continue to try to undress you?

**Mitchell**    Yes, we ended up making love on his couch.

**Kersley**    And did this become a regular occurrence?

**Mitchell**    Oh, yes. After that, Patrick would often turn up late at night, explaining that he told Elizabeth he was out visiting a patient. He made love with such a passion that I was convinced he no longer had a sexual relationship with his wife.

**Kersley**   And how long did this affair go on for?

**Mitchell**   About three months.

**Kersley**   And he asked you to pick up the prescriptions from Wellingborough soon after you started sleeping with him?

**Mitchell**   Within days. But by then Patrick knew only too well that I nearly always visited my parents at the weekend.

**Kersley**   And were these prescriptions ever made out for Mrs Sherwood?

**Mitchell**   No, they were all for private patients.

**Kersley**   Can you recall the date of the first one?

**Mitchell**   Yes. It was about three months before his wife died.

**Kersley**   How can you be so sure?

**Mitchell**   Because I made a diary entry that Patrick had given me a ten-pound note to cover the cost, and there was four pounds change, which I returned to him on the Monday morning.

**Kersley**   But if you were so surprised to be asked to carry out Mr Sherwood's instructions, why didn't you report your misgivings to anyone in authority?

**Mitchell**   Because by then I'd fallen in love with him.

**Kersley**   And did he ever give any hint that he might have fallen in love with you?

**Mitchell**   Oh, yes. Patrick regularly told me he was sick of his wife, and he couldn't wait to be rid of her so he could spend the rest of his life with me. He hated the way she constantly belittled him in front of the staff. He even talked about moving out of Arcadia Mansions, finding a larger apartment and starting a family. I didn't take it too seriously to begin with. But then one night he proposed.

**Kersley**    He asked you to marry him?

**Mitchell**    Yes, he did.

**Kersley**    While his wife was still alive?

**Mitchell**    Yes, it was after we'd made love – I'll never forget it, because he left a few minutes later.

**Kersley**    So would that have been around three in the morning?

**Mitchell**    No, just after ten.

**Kersley**    But you told the court that he usually left around three in the morning, so that no one would realise you were having an affair.

**Mitchell**    Yes, but that night he told me he had to visit a patient in Westminster and he would come back later, which puzzled me.

**Kersley**    Why did it puzzle you, Ms Mitchell?

**Mitchell**    Because he didn't have his doctor's bag with him.

**Kersley**    And did he come back later?

**Mitchell**    Yes, a few minutes after eleven.

**Kersley**    And did you notice any change in him when he returned?

**Mitchell**    Yes, he seemed very nervous. And when I asked if there was a problem, he told me that the patient had died.

**Kersley**    He told you that the patient had died?

**Mitchell**    Yes, I tried to calm him, but he just paced around the room mumbling to himself and then suddenly left without warning.

**Kersley**    And did he ever raise the subject of marriage again?

**Mitchell**   No. Once his wife had died, Patrick refused even to speak to me.

**Kersley**   But this was the man who had regularly shared your bed and even asked you to be his wife.

**Mitchell**   Yes. (*Near to tears.*) Which is why it came as such a terrible shock when he dropped me without any warning. Of course, relationships can come to an end, but that doesn't mean you can't remain on good terms.

**Kersley**   But you did attend Mrs Sherwood's funeral?

**Mitchell**   Yes, but Patrick ignored me and didn't even invite me back to his flat to join the other guests.

**Kersley**   Was there anything else you can remember about the funeral?

**Mitchell**   Yes, I was surprised that Mrs Sherwood was cremated and it made me anxious for the first time.

**Kersley**   What were you anxious about?

**Mitchell**   Well, I began to wonder if Patrick was making sure that no one could ever check what had caused the bruising on her arm.

**Sherwood** *half rises, catches* **Judge**'s *eye and sits back down.*

**Barrington**   My Lord, this is a disgraceful slur on my client. There is absolutely no proof that . . .

**Judge**   I agree, Sir James. The jury will disregard Ms Mitchell's last statement. Ms Mitchell, this court is not interested in your opinions, only in facts. And Mr Kersley, you are as much to blame. You must have known only too well where that question was leading.

**Kersley**   I did, My Lord, but then I considered Mrs Sherwood's cremation to be a fact, and one the jury might even find relevant.

**Judge**   Mr Kersley, you are bordering on impertinence. Stick to facts in future.

**Kersley**   Ms Mitchell, is it a fact that while you continued working at St George's Mr Sherwood began to threaten you?

**Mitchell**   Yes, he did. When I raised the subject of the prescriptions he flew into a rage, warning me that if I mentioned them to anyone, not only would I lose my job at St George's but he would personally make sure that no other hospital would ever employ me again.

**Kersley**   So you decided to leave St George's.

**Mitchell**   I didn't have a lot of choice, as he'd made it abundantly clear that I had no hope of promotion while he remained the head of department.

**Kersley**   So what did you do next?

**Mitchell**   I resigned and took a short holiday abroad. While I was away, a vacancy arose at Wellingborough Cottage Hospital for the position of senior staff nurse. I was delighted when they offered me the post and hoped this would be my chance to start a new life.

**Kersley**   But that didn't prove possible, did it, Ms Mitchell, because Mr Sherwood got in touch with you again. When was that?

**Mitchell**   It must have been about a month after I'd started my new job. He began phoning me at the hospital.

**Sherwood** (*rises*)   I never phoned you. I didn't even know you'd got another job.

**Judge**   Mr Sherwood, this is the last time I shall warn you. If you interrupt again, I will have you taken below as long as Ms Mitchell remains in the witness box. Do I make myself clear?

**Sherwood**   Yes My Lord, but . . .

**Barrington**   My Lord, may I be allowed to have a word with the defendant?

**Judge**    For what purpose, Sir James?

**Barrington**    To leave Mr Sherwood in no doubt of the harm it will do his cause if he is unable to hear all the evidence offered by this particular witness.

**Judge**    Do you have any objection, Mr Kersley?

**Kersley**    If it means I can continue uninterrupted, My Lord, I would welcome it. However, it may be that these unseemly outbursts, repeated by Mr Sherwood at regular intervals despite Your Lordship's continual warnings, will only serve to shed light on the character of the accused and thus assist the jury when the time comes to consider their verdict.

**Barrington**    My Lord, my learned friend can never resist making a speech and this one did indeed shed some light, if not on Mr Sherwood's character, then on the Crown's lack of any real evidence, which they try to cover up by resorting to personal abuse. However, I will have a word with my client My Lord, and warn him of the gravity of your words. (**Barrington** *goes over to the dock.*) Very good, but that was one more interruption than we agreed on, so don't do it again. (**Sherwood** *nods and sits back down,* **Barrington** *returns to his place.*) I'm obliged, My Lord. I think Mr Sherwood now fully understands what is expected of him.

**Judge**    Thank you, Sir James. Carry on, Mr Kersley.

**Kersley**    You were telling us, Ms Mitchell, that Mr Sherwood telephoned you at the hospital – for what purpose?

**Mitchell**    To warn me that the police had begun an investigation into his wife's death and might want to question me about our relationship.

**Kersley**    Really? Did he say anything else?

**Mitchell**    Yes, he begged me not to mention the fact that I'd been with him on the night his wife died, as he had already come up with a more convincing alibi.

**Kersley**  Why would he need another alibi, if he had been with you?

**Mitchell**  Because he didn't want the police to know that we'd been having an affair.

**Kersley**  And how did you respond to this request?

**Mitchell**  I told him to go to hell and rang off.

**Kersley**  Did he call again that day?

**Mitchell**  Yes, about an hour later, but I refused to speak to him.

**Kersley**  How did you avoid it?

**Mitchell**  I made some excuse to Sister about not feeling well, and went home early. But that night I was so distressed I just couldn't get to sleep, so in the morning I told my parents everything.

**Kersley**  And it was your father, Councillor Mitchell, who left you in no doubt as to where your responsibility lay?

**Mitchell**  Yes. He advised me to tell the police everything I knew, otherwise I could be an accessory to the crime and just as guilty as he was.

**Kersley**  And when the police got in touch with you, you immediately volunteered a statement?

**Mitchell**  Yes, I did.

**Kersley**  And has Mr Sherwood tried to contact you again since you made that statement?

**Mitchell**  He never stops phoning, sometimes twice a day, but I haven't spoken to him since that morning he rang the hospital. (**Sherwood** *rises but then sits back down.*)

**Kersley**  And despite all that you've been put through these last six months, you still have no regrets about taking your father's advice?

**Mitchell**    None whatsoever. My only regret . . . (*She hesitates.*)

**Kersley**    Yes, Ms Mitchell? Your only regret?

**Mitchell** (*stares at* **Sherwood**)    . . . is that I ever agreed to collect those prescriptions for him in the first place.

**Kersley**    No more questions, My Lord.

**Judge**    Your witness, Sir James.

**Barrington**    Thank you, My Lord. Allow me to begin, Ms Mitchell, with the subject of the prescriptions. Can I confirm that you were aware that Potassium Chloride was classified as a controlled drug?

**Mitchell**    Yes, of course I was.

**Barrington**    So you would have had to sign for them?

**Mitchell**    Yes, I signed for all six of them, and as the prescriptions are in the court's safe keeping, you can check for yourself.

**Barrington**    I already have, from my photocopies. I just wanted you to confirm that it was your signature on the originals.

**Usher** *shows her the originals.*

**Mitchell**    Yes, that is my signature.

**Barrington**    Then perhaps you won't mind writing your name on the Usher's pad so that the jury can be left in no doubt. (*She signs her signature with her left hand and the* **Usher** *shows the pad to* **Barrington**.) Yes, there is no doubt it is your signature. (*He checks the prescriptions.*) You said in your statement to the police that Mr Sherwood only gave you those prescriptions on a Friday evening, just as you were about to leave for the weekend.

**Mitchell**    Yes, that's correct.

**Barrington**   Then perhaps you can explain why, of the six prescriptions (*Holds them up.*) one is dated on a Tuesday, two on a Wednesday, two on a Thursday, leaving only one made out on a Friday, which was the one found in Mr Sherwood's bag. (*He places five of them to one side.*)

**Mitchell**   I said nothing about when they were made out, only when he handed them to me for collection and that was always on a Friday evening.

**Barrington**   How convenient. Unless, of course, you held on to them until you went home for the weekend.

**Mitchell**   Why should I do that?

**Barrington**   Why indeed, unless, of course, you had your own reason for wanting to implicate Mr Sherwood, which brings me on to this mythical relationship you claim he began.

**Mitchell**   It wasn't mythical and he certainly began it.

**Barrington**   You say he showered you with presents, sent you flowers, took you out to dinner – even occasionally to the theatre.

**Mitchell**   Yes, he did.

**Barrington**   Do you have any proof that these presents ever existed?

**Mitchell**   No, of course I don't. The flowers have died and I've eaten all the chocolates.

**Barrington**   Now that is convenient. So you're asking the court to believe that all these presents were in one way or another, how can I put this, biodegradable? And were these dinners always at restaurants where he wouldn't be recognised?

**Mitchell**   Yes, that was the idea. Patrick said it wouldn't look good if we were seen together while his wife was still alive.

**Barrington**    Can you name any of these restaurants?

**Mitchell** (*considers this*)    Not off the top of my head, no. But then we never went back to the same one twice, although I do remember we once ate in Fulham.

**Barrington**    And after you'd had dinner at these restaurants you can't name, you would sometimes go on to the theatre?

**Mitchell**    Yes, on at least two occasions.

**Barrington**    So you must be able to name at least two of the plays?

**Mitchell** (*hesitates*)    Not immediately. After all, it was over a year ago, but I remember one of them was by Tom Stoppard – and in any case I kept the programmes.

**Kersley** *whispers to* **Ashton**, *who makes a note.*

**Barrington**    And after he'd taken you to the theatre, would he then drive you home?

**Mitchell**    Yes, he always took me home.

**Barrington**    And on one occasion he asked if he could join you for coffee?

**Mitchell**    Yes, that's right.

**Barrington**    And until then, he hadn't tried to do anything that could be described as improper?

**Mitchell**    No, but two weeks later he grabbed me at the staff party and started kissing me under the mistletoe, and then he put his hand on my . . .

**Barrington**    Quite. Where was the mistletoe hanging, Ms Mitchell?

**Mitchell** (*hesitates*)    From a light in the middle of the room.

**Barrington**    From a light in the middle of the room. Let me see if I can picture this, Ms Mitchell. He had one hand on your breast, while at the same time trying to kiss you, in

the middle of a crowded room, in front of all his colleagues
and your friends.

**Mitchell**    Yes. It was very embarrassing.

**Barrington**    Not embarrassing enough to stop you letting
him take you home and then end up in bed with him.

**Mitchell**    I felt sorry for him.

**Barrington**    Ah, yes, I remember, it was raining. Have
you any idea, Ms Mitchell, how unlikely this story is
sounding?

**Mitchell**    It's the truth and he knows it.

**Barrington**    Well, then let's continue with this morality
fable, shall we? The following morning Mr Sherwood called
you into his office, locked the door and started trying to
undo your uniform?

**Mitchell**    Yes, he did.

**Barrington**    And then he made love to you on his couch?

**Mitchell**    Yes, just as I described it.

**Barrington**    What time of day was that?

**Mitchell**    I don't remember exactly.

**Barrington**    Well how about vaguely – eight o'clock, nine
o'clock, ten o'clock?

**Mitchell**    I think it must have been about nine thirty. Yes,
it was just after we'd completed the early-morning rounds.

**Barrington**    So you're asking the court to believe that
having left you, exhausted, at three in the morning, he then
made love to you again at nine thirty?

**Mitchell**    Yes, and I wasn't the only nurse who'd been
subjected to 'after-rounds' sex.

**Barrington**    Strange, because I don't see any of those
nurses on the list of Crown witnesses.

**Mitchell**    They didn't want to know, once they realised the police were involved.

**Barrington**    Strange how everybody and everything disappears whenever you're involved. And after this romp on the couch, he regularly made love to you in his office and sometimes spent the night with you back at your flat?

**Mitchell**    No, he never stayed the night. He always left around three in the morning. He didn't want anyone to find out that we were having an affair.

**Barrington**    And you say that this relationship went on for several weeks?

**Mitchell**    Over three months.

**Barrington**    And you would also have us believe that on one occasion, he asked you to marry him?

**Mitchell**    Yes, he did.

**Barrington**    Was this at a restaurant you can't remember, or after a play you don't recall?

**Mitchell**    No, I remember the occasion well; it's not something a girl is likely to forget. You see, he proposed to me on the night his wife died.

**Barrington** (*sharply*)    How could you possibly have known it was the night his wife was going to die?

**Mitchell**    Obviously I didn't know until the following morning. But I'll never forget his words after we'd made love – 'Elizabeth won't be around for much longer, so we ought to start thinking about our future together.'

**Barrington**    Elizabeth. Did you ever meet Mrs Sherwood?

**Mitchell**    Only when she came to pick up her husband from the hospital.

**Barrington**    So you never visited her at the flat?

**Mitchell**    No, why should I do that?

**Barrington**    To help her with her injections, perhaps?

**Mitchell**    No, I've never been to Arcadia Mansions.

**Barrington**    Arcadia Mansions. So it wasn't you who was at the apartment when Mrs Sherwood said, 'How did you get in?'

**Mitchell**    No, I was at home all that evening.

**Barrington**    Alone?

**Mitchell**    No, Patrick joined me around eight o'clock. I cooked dinner for him and then we made love in front of the fire. Perhaps you'd like me to go into the details?

**Barrington**    Yes, I would, Ms Mitchell, because if this relationship was as intimate as you say, you'll be able to tell the court if Mr Sherwood has any scars, birth marks or even unusual habits that only someone who was so intimate with him would be aware of.

**Mitchell** (*triumphantly*)    Yes, I can. Patrick has a small burn on his right arm (*Touches her right forearm.*) which you can only see when he takes his shirt off.

**Barrington**    'A small burn on his right arm . . . Only when he takes his shirt off.' (*He writes down as a quote.*) Anything else?

**Mitchell** (*considers this*)    Yes, whenever he took me out on a date, he would remove his wedding ring and when we made love he would always insist on putting out the light. And, oh yes, his great passion is sailing. He keeps a small boat at Burnham, which he takes out most weekends.

**Barrington**    One could hardly call this list of mundane trivia intimate knowledge. You know, Ms Mitchell, this is beginning to sound less and less like an affair and more and more like wishful thinking.

**Mitchell**    I can assure you it was real.

**Barrington**    I have no doubt you wanted it to be real.

**Mitchell**    What do you mean by that?

**Barrington**   Simply that no one was better placed than you to take advantage of a man who was nursing a dying wife. But he rejected your advances, which made you bitter and resentful. And then, after his wife died, you come up with this cock-and-bull story about Wellingborough, only too aware of how hard it would be for Mr Sherwood to prove his innocence.

**Kersley**   My Lord, I think I must have fallen asleep, because the last thing I remember was my learned friend cross-examining this witness, and I seem to have woken up in the middle of his closing speech. Can your Lordship advise me, have I missed any significant questions?

**Judge**   No, but you have improperly interrupted defence counsel, just as – I suspect – he was about to ask one. Please continue, Sir James.

**Barrington**   If it is a question my learned friend demands, then a question he will get. My Lord, could Ms Mitchell be shown exhibit twenty-three?

**Judge**   Yes, Usher. (*He nods the* **Usher** *to hold up the glove.*)

**Barrington**   Ms Mitchell, do you know what this is?

**Mitchell**   Yes, of course I do, it's a rubber glove.

**Barrington**   Used for hygienic purposes when administering an injection.

**Mitchell**   Or for washing the dishes.

**Barrington**   It was found on the floor of the Sherwoods' kitchen the night his wife died.

**Mitchell**   So what does that prove?

**Barrington**   It's a left-handed glove, Ms Mitchell – are you, by any chance, left-handed?

**Mitchell**   No, I'm right-handed.

**Barrington**   Strange, because when you signed your signature on the Usher's pad only a few moments ago, you did so with your left hand. Would you care to try on the glove, Ms Mitchell?

**Kersley**   My Lord, this is outrageous, it's not Ms Mitchell who is on trial here.

**Judge**   I agree, Mr Kersley. Sir James, your job is to defend Mr Sherwood, not to prosecute Ms Mitchell. Stick to your brief.

**Barrington**   As you wish, My Lord. But I do hope my learned friend will not object to me asking Ms Mitchell about the phone calls she claims Mr Sherwood made to her after she had left St George's.

**Mitchell**   He did call me, again and again.

**Barrington**   Again and again. Then how is it that BT are unable to trace a single call to Wellingborough Cottage Hospital from either Mr Sherwood's office, his home or his mobile?

**Mitchell**   He could have called me from a phone box.

**Barrington**   Oh, I see, so several times a day he just popped out of the operating theatre to phone boxes all over London to plead with you to keep quiet about your affair.

**Mitchell**   Yes, he did.

**Barrington**   You know, Ms Mitchell, these calls are beginning to sound like the presents, the flowers, the restaurants and the theatre, absolutely no proof of anything actually taking place – which brings me on to the statement that you made to the police following Mrs Sherwood's death.

**Mitchell**   Yes, I made a voluntary statement to Chief Inspector Payne.

**Barrington**   You did indeed, Ms Mitchell, but what I want to know is what you mean by the word voluntary? Was it an unsolicited statement? Did you, for example, visit a police station and offer to assist them with their enquiries?

**Mitchell**    It wasn't quite like that.

**Barrington**    It wasn't anything like that, was it, Ms Mitchell? The only reason you volunteered a statement was because your father, Councillor Mitchell, had warned you that if you didn't, you might well be implicated yourself. And correct me if I'm wrong, you didn't make that statement until after Chief Inspector Payne had contacted you some weeks later?

**Mitchell**    I volunteered a statement immediately he contacted me.

**Barrington**    Yes, but why didn't you contact the police immediately following Mrs Sherwood's death? Why leave it until Inspector Payne had got in touch with you?

**Mitchell** (*voice rising*)    Because I didn't have any proof. It would only have been my word against his.

**Barrington**    At last we come down to the reality of this case – you didn't have any proof. It's simply your word against his. The truth is, Ms Mitchell, that your word isn't worth the Usher's pad it's written on because there never was any relationship between you and the defendant.

**Mitchell** (*breaking down sobbing*)    Yes, there was. We were lovers and he even asked me to be his wife.

**Barrington**    Did you accept his proposal?

**Mitchell**    Yes, I did.

**Barrington**    So you must have been in love with him at the time?

**Mitchell**    Yes, I was at the time.

**Barrington**    So how do you feel about him now, Ms Mitchell?

**Mitchell**    I loathe him.

**Barrington**    You loathe him?

**Mitchell** (*voice rising*)    Yes, I loathe him. When he needed me, nothing was too much trouble for him, but once I'd served my purpose he dumped me as if I had never existed.

**Barrington**    Try not to raise your voice too much, Ms Mitchell. Otherwise the jury might begin to suspect that . . .

**Mitchell** (*still sobbing*)    I don't care what they . . .

**Kersley**    My Lord, I must object. Do these attacks on Ms Mitchell have any real purpose other than to intimidate?

**Judge**    Do they, Sir James?

**Barrington**    They most certainly do, My Lord, their purpose is to ensure that an innocent man doesn't have to spend the rest of his life in gaol on the evidence of a jealous, vindictive woman who couldn't get her own way. Ms Mitchell, if you are going to persist in claiming that Mr Sherwood seduced you, I must remind you, before you answer my next question, that you are still under oath. (*He pauses.*) Was Mr Sherwood the first person you had an affair with at St George's? (**Jarvis** *hands him blank sheet of paper that the audience can see is blank.*)

**Mitchell** (*hesitates*)    There may have been one other.

**Barrington** (*stares down at blank sheet*)    Only one other, Ms Mitchell?

**Mitchell**    Well, over a period of five years, perhaps two.

**Barrington** (*continues to stare at sheet*)    Two?

**Mitchell** (*she hesitates*)    Possibly three.

**Barrington** (*slowly*)    Or four, or five, or . . .

**Mitchell**    No – three.

**Barrington**    And were any or all three of these paramours also doctors or surgeons, by any chance?

**Mitchell**    Yes, but the first one was years ago and didn't last that long.

**Barrington**    Are you certain, of that Ms Mitchell?

**Mitchell**    Yes, I am, but then I feel sure even you can remember when you lost your virginity, Sir James.

**Barrington** (*continues to stare at the blank sheet of paper*)    But your second and third affairs lasted a considerably longer time, didn't they?

**Mitchell**    Yes, but they were over long before Patrick began courting me.

**Barrington** (*voice rising*)    But isn't it the truth, Ms Mitchell, that having failed to snare one doctor, you were willing to go to any lengths to catch another?

**Mitchell**    No, that is not the truth. The truth is that Patrick told me that he loved me and asked me to be his wife, and I can prove it.

**Barrington**    Like you can prove he gave you prescriptions only on a Friday evening, like you can prove that he showered you with presents that no longer exist, like you can prove which restaurants he took you to, but you can't remember their names, like you can prove which theatres you attended, but can't recall the titles of the plays, like you can prove he telephoned you again and again, but there's no trace of any calls, like you can prove . . .

**Mitchell**    That he made me pregnant. (**Barrington** *is stopped in his tracks*.) And when I told him I was going to have his baby, he begged me to have an abortion. (*She looks defiantly at* **Sherwood**.) And I only agreed to his demands because I wasn't willing to give birth to the bastard of a murderer.

CURTAIN

# Act Three

## Scene One

*The following day.*
*The **Jury Bailiff** walks through the door and addresses the audience. Clock shows 9.45.*

**Jury Bailiff**  Good morning Ladies and Gentlemen of the Jury. Today it is the turn of Sir James Barrington to take up the cudgels on behalf of the Defence. I am unable to give you any guidance as to the witnesses he intends to call (*He glances at his clipboard.*) as no names appear on the list. This, of course, may be a ruse by Sir James to keep the Prosecution guessing. Or it may simply be that following Ms Mitchell's evidence yesterday, Sir James has not yet decided whether to put Mr Sherwood, in the witness box, where he would have to face cross-examination by Mr Kersley. It is, of course, not compulsory under English law for a defendant to take the stand. However, if he does not, inferences of guilt may be drawn. Ladies and Gentlemen of the Jury, if you are ready, we will return to Court Number One.

*He steps through the door; when the lights come up, we are back in Court Number One. Everyone is in place awaiting the **Judge** and jury.*

**Ashton**  Do you think he'll put Sherwood in the box?

**Kersley**  I wouldn't. Always quit while you're ahead.

**Ashton**  You think he's ahead, after all you achieved yesterday?

**Kersley**  Yes, I do. A trial can be going your way and then suddenly one piece of evidence will derail you. Did you see the faces of the jury when they discovered that Ms Mitchell was left-handed. Doubt must have crept into their minds. No, we must hope that he puts Sherwood in the witness box. And if he does, I'll need those two theatre programmes.

**Ashton**   Ms Mitchell dropped them off in chambers this morning. They're both in the envelope.

**Kersley**   Good.

**Barrington**   Have you had a chance to speak to our client this morning?

**Jarvis**   He was consuming gallons of black coffee, wondering if you had come to a decision about putting him in the witness box.

**Barrington**   I haven't been left with a lot of choice after Mitchell's revelation yesterday. It was a bad mistake on my part, Andrew. What did you learn from it?

**Jarvis**   Not to ask one question too many.

**Barrington**   A barrister's worst nightmare. If I had stopped the moment she admitted to having affairs with three other doctors, the jury would not have been quite so sure about the rest of her evidence. Why in heaven's name didn't Sherwood tell us about the abortion in the first place?

**Jarvis**   Perhaps he didn't know himself and I have a feeling that Kersley was as surprised as we were.

**Barrington**   Don't you believe it. Kersley rehearsed her down to the last syllable.

**Jarvis**   All the same, I thought he was impressive yesterday . . .

**Barrington**   (*He looks across at* **Kersley** *who is talking to* **Ashton**) Yes he was, damn the man – but that was yesterday. We still have one piece of evidence that Kersley doesn't know about. If he did, Mitchell would have revealed it, and that would have ended any chance of us winning this case.

*Three knocks to announce the arrival of the* **Judge**.

**Usher**   Be upstanding in the court. All persons having anything to do before my Lords, the Queen's Justices, draw near and give your attendance. God save the Queen.

*The **Judge** enters and takes his place. All bow to the **Judge** who returns the bow.*

**Usher**   Bring up the prisoner.

**Judge**   Sir James, are you ready to open the Defence case?

**Barrington**   Yes, My Lord, I am. May it please your Lordship, Members of the Jury, I rose this morning with a heavy heart, only too aware of the responsibility that rests upon my shoulders. For it has been left for me to convince the Jury that Mr Sherwood, far from being consumed with murderous intent as Ms Mitchell would have us all believe, is in fact a simple decent man who has devoted his life to the service of others.

But Members of the Jury, for you to be convinced that this man is capable of murder, you have to ask yourself what was the motive, because all crimes must, in the end, have a motive. And, perhaps even more important, where is the evidence to convict Mr Sherwood? Because the evidence in this case has been at best circumstantial, and at worst, prejudicial.

Members of the Jury, English law does not demand that a defendant should appear in the witness box and it is right that it does not do so, but so determined is Mr Sherwood to clear his good name, that he is willing to face cross-examination and be judged by his peers.

My Lord, I call Mr Patrick Sherwood.

**Usher**   Mr Sherwood

**Kersley** *smiles as* **Sherwood** *leaves the dock, walks across the courtroom and enters the witness box.*

**Usher**   Please take the testament in your right hand and read from the card.

**Sherwood**   I swear by Almighty God that the evidence I shall give shall be the truth, the whole truth and nothing but the truth.

**Barrington**   Your name is Patrick Hugh Sherwood and you reside at twenty-two Cadogan Villas in the county of London?

**Sherwood**   Yes, I do.

**Barrington**   You are presently a senior consultant, head of the Cardio Thoracic Unit at St George's, and a Fellow of the Royal College of Surgeons?

**Sherwood**   That is correct.

**Barrington**   Your life-long hobby has been sailing and until the age of forty-five you were a surgeon captain in the Royal Naval Volunteer Reserve?

**Sherwood**   Yes, and I still keep a small boat at Burnham, which my wife . . . my late wife and I used to sail at weekends.

**Barrington**   In 1982 you were called up as a reservist to serve in the Falklands, where you performed over a hundred operations in twenty-nine days.

**Sherwood**   I have no idea how many operations I performed.

**Barrington**   My Lord, over a hundred were the words mentioned in dispatches by the fleet commander. Now I'd like to begin, Mr Sherwood, with your relationship with your wife. How long were you married?

**Sherwood**   Just over seventeen years.

**Barrington**   And was your marriage a happy one?

**Sherwood**   I adored Elizabeth; no one will ever be able to replace her.

**Barrington**   When was it that you first discovered your wife had a heart problem?

**Sherwood**   The first hint came in 1997, when Elizabeth complained of loss of breath, and of feeling pains in her chest, and left arm. These are the classic signs of a minor heart attack, so I took her into St George's and carried out some routine tests.

**Barrington**   And what did those tests reveal?

**Sherwood**   That her heartbeat was irregular and she was suffering from an arrhythmia.

**Barrington**   Did you consider this curable at the time?

**Sherwood**   Oh, yes, I deal with this sort of problem every day, and as long as a patient is willing to be disciplined with their diet, sensible about taking exercise and, if it applies, give up smoking, then there's no reason why they shouldn't live to an old age.

**Barrington**   So what did you do next?

**Sherwood**   I put her on a programme of medication that was approved by her GP and confirmed by the brightest young specialist on my staff.

**Barrington**   And once she had begun that programme, did her health start to improve?

**Sherwood**   No, she continued to complain about loss of breath and feeling tired, which caused me to doubt my own diagnosis.

**Barrington**   So what did you do about it?

**Sherwood**   I got in touch with Sir Magdi Yacoub at the Brompton Hospital. He's the leading authority in my field and I was keen to seek a second opinion.

**Barrington**   And what was his judgement?

**Sherwood**   He was puzzled. He could find no fault with my diagnosis and suggested that Elizabeth be put on a special fat-free diet.

**Barrington**   And did you at last see some improvement?

**Sherwood**    No, her health continued to deteriorate and during the last few months I couldn't get her to leave the flat, even to go for a short walk.

**Barrington**    And she finally collapsed on the evening of March the twenty-first 1999, and was taken into hospital, where she died of cardiac arrest a few hours later.

**Sherwood** (*bows his head*)    Yes and I'll never forgive myself for not being by her side.

**Barrington**    Looking back over that last year, do you think you could have done any more?

**Sherwood**    I ask myself the same question a hundred times every day, and I think I can honestly say that I did everything in my power to prolong Elizabeth's life.

**Barrington**    But the Crown would have us believe that over a period of three months, you instructed Ms Mitchell to pick up several ampoules of Potassium Chloride from a chemist in Wellingborough for the sole purpose of poisoning your wife.

**Sherwood**    The Crown only has Ms Mitchell's word for that.

**Barrington**    But your signature is on all the prescriptions.

**Sherwood**    And hundreds of others like it, Sir James, but it's the first time I've been arrested and charged with murder.

**Barrington**    Then why did you ask her to have them made up in Wellingborough?

**Sherwood**    I didn't – she could have collected those prescriptions from the hospital pharmacy whenever it suited her.

**Barrington**    And now I would like to address the Crown's suggestion that after your wife died, it was you who gave the instruction to have her body cremated. Is that true, Mr Sherwood?

**Sherwood**   No. I'd been against the idea right from the start. If it hadn't been for a codicil in Elizabeth's will, she would have been buried in the family plot at Highgate cemetery. And if only she had been, I wouldn't be standing in front of you today.

**Barrington**   Quite so. Which brings me on to Ms Mitchell, and the one question on which this whole case rests. Whether you did, or did not, have an affair with this lady – for the purpose of using her as part of a well-thought-out plan to poison your wife. So let me ask you straight away, Mr Sherwood, what was your relationship with Ms Mitchell?

**Sherwood**   Entirely professional. On the rare occasions we met outside the hospital, it would have been at gatherings where other members of staff were present.

**Barrington**   Did you ever flirt with Ms Mitchell?

**Sherwood**   I flirt with all the nurses in my department, Sir James.

**Barrington**   You flirt with all the nurses in your department?

**Sherwood**   When you work on a cardiac unit you come into contact with death every day, which naturally causes relationships to be quite intense. One's moods swing from being morose to flippant and sometimes to just downright silly.

**Barrington**   But Ms Mitchell claims that you gave her presents, sent her flowers, took her to restaurants and, on at least two occasions, accompanied her to the theatre?

**Sherwood**   I think on one occasion I did pass on a box of chocolates to Ms Mitchell that had been given to me by a patient, but as for all her other suggestions, they are nothing more than fantasy.

**Barrington**    She went on to tell the court that after having dinner together you would then drive her home. Is that also fantasy?

**Sherwood**    It's not only fantasy, Sir James, it's simply not possible.

**Barrington**    I'm not sure I understand, Mr Sherwood.

**Sherwood**    It's quite hard to drive someone home when you don't own a car.

**Barrington**    But you could have borrowed a car from the hospital, even hired one.

**Sherwood**    Yes, I could have done, if I had a driving licence.

**Barrington**    You don't have a driving licence?

**Sherwood**    No and I've never had one. Elizabeth used to drive me everywhere.

**Barrington**    But even if you didn't drive Ms Mitchell home, she claimed that you regularly joined her in her flat for coffee.

**Sherwood**    I never drink coffee, Sir James, gallons of tea, but never coffee.

**Barrington**    I must now ask you about Ms Mitchell's claims that you told her not to inform the police that you had been with her on the night your wife died, because you had come up with a more convincing alibi. How do you *answer* that charge?

**Sherwood**    There is no need to answer it, Sir James, because I don't even know where she lives.

**Barrington**    But Mr Sherwood, you're on trial for murder. Why not admit to having an affair, rather than risk going to prison for the rest of your life?

**Sherwood**    Because we didn't have an affair.

**Barrington**    But you did go as far as kissing her on one occasion?

**Sherwood**    Yes I did – it was at the staff Christmas party. I'd drunk a little too much, and regretted it immediately. I apologised and left soon afterwards.

**Barrington**    So as far as you were concerned, that was an end of the matter?

**Sherwood**    It would have been if I hadn't asked her to come to my office the following morning.

**Barrington**    Why did you do that?

**Sherwood**    I wanted to apologise more formally.

**Barrington**    And what was her reaction?

**Sherwood**    She said there was no need to apologise as she had enjoyed it. She then locked the door and started to unbutton her uniform.

**Barrington**    How did you react?

**Sherwood**    I went straight to the door, unlocked it, held it open and waited for her to leave.

**Barrington**    Did she do so?

**Sherwood**    Yes, she did, but I'll never forget her words as she stormed out of the room: 'Mr Sherwood, you will live to regret this.'

**Barrington**    What did you imagine she meant by that?

**Sherwood**    I thought she might report me to the hospital board, even to an industrial tribunal.

**Barrington**    And did she do so?

**Sherwood**    No, she was far more devious than that. But even I couldn't have imagined she would claim I was with her the night my wife died.

**Barrington**    Where were you that night, Mr Sherwood?

**Sherwood**   I was out on an emergency call visiting a patient in Westminster.

**Barrington**   So why isn't that patient in court today to verify your story?

**Sherwood**   Because he died later that night.

**Barrington**   And what was the time entered on the death certificate?

**Sherwood**   10.27 p.m.

**Barrington**   And who signed that death certificate?

**Sherwood**   I did.

**Barrington**   So if it was signed at 10.27 p.m., you would not have needed a more convincing alibi, as Ms Mitchell suggested.

**Sherwood**   Ms Mitchell seems to think I could have been in two places at once.

**Barrington**   Quite. So finally, let me ask you, Mr Sherwood, how do you answer Ms Mitchell's damning accusation that you used her as a courier over a period of three months, to collect ampoules of Potassium Chloride in order to poison your wife?

**Sherwood**   Sir James, if I had wanted to poison my wife, I could have picked up any amount of drugs from the hospital pharmacy, without ever involving Ms Mitchell. No, the truth is that during that unhappy year I tended to my wife's every need, often neglecting other patients. I only wish I'd been as successful with Elizabeth as I have been with some of them.

**Barrington**   No further questions, My Lord.

**Judge**   Do you wish to cross-examine, Mr Kersley?

**Kersley**   I most certainly do, My Lord. Mr Sherwood, much as we enjoyed the description of your wedded bliss, I suspect the time has now come for all of us in this courtroom to return to the real world. Let me begin by asking you when you first met Ms Mitchell?

**Sherwood**    It must have been when she was transferred to the cardiac unit.

**Kersley**    And did you find her attractive?

**Sherwood**    No, I didn't think of her in that way.

**Kersley**    So it wasn't love at first sight?

**Sherwood**    Or second sight, Mr Kersley.

**Kersley**    So it was some time later that you fell under her spell?

**Sherwood**    I never fell under her spell.

**Kersley**    Ah. So she was correct in suggesting that you were the pursuer and she the pursued in this relationship?

**Sherwood**    There never was a relationship, Mr Kersley.

**Kersley**    I shall return to the proof of that relationship later, Mr Sherwood.

**Sherwood**    And I shall continue to deny it.

**Kersley**    I'll look forward to that. So let me turn to something you can't deny. Where do you live?

**Sherwood**    Twenty-two Cadogan Villas.

**Kersley**    So when did you move out of your flat in Wimbledon?

**Sherwood**    About a year ago.

**Kersley**    And how much did it cost to purchase a penthouse in Chelsea?

**Sherwood**    I don't remember exactly.

**Kersley**    Come, come, Mr Sherwood, I think every one of us knows exactly what we paid for the home we live in, especially if we bought it less than a year ago. I repeat, how much did it cost to purchase a penthouse in Chelsea?

**Sherwood**   Around eight hundred thousand pounds.

**Kersley**   Wouldn't eight hundred and thirty-seven thousand be more accurate?

**Sherwood**   Possibly.

**Kersley**   So you must have won the lottery? Or did you inherit it?

**Sherwood**   Neither. My wife left few assets in her will. By the time I had finished paying death duties I received less than twenty thousand pounds.

**Kersley**   Well, that would just about cover the stamp duty on twenty-two Cadogan villas, so I must therefore ask you what the current salary is for a surgeon at St George's?

**Sherwood**   Just over ninety thousand pounds a year.

**Kersley**   How many people earning ninety thousand pounds a year can afford to purchase a penthouse in Chelsea for eight hundred and thirty-seven thousand pounds? I feel sure you're about to tell us that there's another simple explanation.

**Sherwood**   Yes, there is. Some years ago I took out a joint life insurance policy on my wife and myself.

**Kersley**   Some years ago. Wouldn't March 1997 be more precise?

**Sherwood**   That is some years ago, Mr Kersley.

**Kersley**   But it's only some weeks before your wife suffered her first heart attack – 'the first hint came in 1997, my wife complained of loss of breath, pains in her left arm and chest . . .' – And what was the value of the policy?

**Sherwood**   A million pounds.

**Kersley**    One million pounds. And would I be right in thinking that the life insurance company are refusing to settle the amount until the result of this trial is known?

**Barrington**    My Lord, that can only be speculation.

**Judge**    I agree, Sir James. Mr Kersley, unless you can provide evidence, move on.

**Kersley**    Mr Sherwood, has the life insurance company settled the full amount?

**Judge**    Mr Kersley.

**Kersley**    I apologise, My Lord. However, I do hope my learned friend will consider one million pounds a large enough sum to constitute the motive he was searching for.

**Sherwood**    No amount of money would constitute a motive for harming my wife.

**Kersley**    Is that right? Then why did you tell Ms Mitchell that you were sick of the way she continually belittled you in front of the hospital staff and how you longed to be rid of her?

**Sherwood**    My Lord, do I have to answer such a ridiculous suggestion?

**Judge**    Yes, I'm afraid you do, Mr Sherwood.

**Sherwood**    Of course I didn't want to be rid of my wife. She was the only woman I've ever cared for.

**Kersley**    Then why did you seek solace in the arms of another?

**Sherwood**    I did no such thing.

**Kersley**    So when Ms Mitchell informed the court that your wife had refused to make love to you for several years, was that also untrue?

**Sherwood**    How could she possibly know?

**Kersley**   Oh, I see, you regularly made love to your wife, did you, Mr Sherwood? (**Sherwood** *hesitates.*) Your silence speaks volumes and, more importantly, supplies us with yet another motive.

**Sherwood**   It does no such thing. When will you work out that when it comes to my private life, Ms Mitchell simply made it up?

**Kersley**   Well, then, let's consider something Ms Mitchell couldn't have made up – your wife's desire to be cremated. Mr Sherwood, your wife's will – was it written in her own hand?

**Sherwood**   No, it was typed.

**Kersley**   Typed by whom, may I ask?

**Sherwood** (*hesitates*)   I think I may have typed it, but it was signed and duly witnessed.

**Kersley**   So who witnessed the document?

**Sherwood**   Mr Webster, the porter at Arcadia Mansions.

**Kersley**   A man who – by his own admission – could neither read nor write.

**Sherwood**   It wasn't necessary for him to read or write, he was only witnessing my wife's signature.

**Kersley**   So just a few days before your wife dies she suddenly adds a codicil to her will stating that she wishes to be cremated. No doubt my learned friend will once again casually dismiss this piece of evidence as circumstantial and coincidental, rather than using his favourite words, 'how convenient'.

**Barrington**   My Lord, I'm enjoying this speech immensely, as I feel sure you are, but if it is to continue for much longer, perhaps my client might be allowed to sit down?

**Kersley**    When I've finished, your client may well need to sit down. Mr Sherwood, you told the court that you consulted the eminent surgeon Sir Magdi Yacoub about your wife's condition and he put her on a special fat-free diet.

**Sherwood**    Sir Magdi has written to the court confirming as much.

**Kersley**    But wasn't that exactly what you were hoping to achieve, so that when your wife died, you would be able to show that she had been treated by the nation's leading specialist and therefore no awkward questions would be asked?

**Sherwood**    That's ridiculous. How could I be expected to fool the leading authority in the land?

**Kersley**    Because you neglected to inform him about the six ampoules of Potassium Chloride that later mysteriously disappeared. Or are you at last going to tell us what really happened to them?

**Sherwood**    Mr Kersley, in a hospital as large as St George's, thousands of drugs are dispensed every week. How could I be expected to account for every one of them the following day, let alone a year later?

**Kersley**    Let alone a year later. So why don't we turn to something you should be able to account for – even a year later – namely your actions on the night your wife died. Did you pour the glass of wine found by her side?

**Sherwood**    Yes, I did, but that was before I left the flat.

**Kersley**    So it must have been you who added the sedative that DCI Payne described as three times the normal dosage?

**Sherwood**    No it was not. My wife was in the habit of taking sedatives, so it could have been a mistake.

**Kersley**   Or part of your plan, like leaving the kitchen window open.

**Sherwood**   Why should I do that?

**Kersley**   So that you could return to your flat without being seen by the porter.

**Sherwood**   How often do you have to be told? I didn't return to the flat. I was visiting a patient.

**Kersley**   In that case, why did you forget to take your doctor's bag?

**Sherwood**   I didn't forget it.

**Kersley**   But Mr Webster testified that he saw you leaving the building without it.

**Sherwood**   Only moments ago you dismissed Mr Webster as unfit to witness my wife's signature.

**Kersley**   So are you now saying that you did have your doctor's bag with you when you left Arcadia Mansions?

**Sherwood**   You don't need a doctor's bag if all you have to do is sign a death certificate.

**Kersley**   And you certainly wouldn't have needed a doctor's bag if you were visiting your mistress in Tooting, unless, of course, it was full of condoms.

**Barrington** (*leaps up*)   My Lord . . .

**Judge**   Yes, yes, Sir James. Mr Kersley, do try to remember that you are at the Old Bailey and not back in the House of Commons.

**Kersley**   I do apologise, My Lord. So, wherever you were, Mr Sherwood – visiting a patient in Westminster without your doctor's bag, or making love to your mistress in Tooting . . .

**Sherwood**   I don't have a mistress – in Tooting or anywhere else for that matter.

**Kersley**    But Ms Mitchell told the court that after you made love, you left her at ten o'clock – without your doctor's bag – and returned an hour later in a nervous state.

**Sherwood**    I wasn't in a nervous state.

**Kersley**    Because you thought you'd got away with it.

**Sherwood**    Because I wasn't with her in the first place.

**Kersley**    Then where were you at 10.27?

**Sherwood**    I was in Westminster signing a death certificate and that certificate is in the court's possession.

**Kersley**    Indeed it is, but isn't it common practice to fill in a death certificate the following day?

**Sherwood**    Not in my department, it isn't.

**Kersley**    Then if it wasn't you who returned to your flat, how do you explain your wife's words – 'How did you get in?'

**Sherwood** (*pause*)    She could have been addressing Mr Webster.

**Kersley**    But he walked in through the front door. I don't think so, Mr Sherwood.

**Sherwood**    Then she must have been surprised by an intruder.

**Kersley**    Rather familiar words for an intruder I would have thought. But singularly appropriate for a husband who had returned unexpectedly and not via the front door. 'How did you get in?'

**Sherwood**    But I didn't return unexpectedly via any door.

**Kersley**    Then via the fire escape, perhaps?

**Sherwood**    Or the fire escape.

**Kersley**    Then how about the kitchen window?

**Sherwood**    Or the kitchen window.

**Kersley**    Then who slipped back into the kitchen just before Mr Webster came in?

**Sherwood**    It could have been the wind that caused the door to slam.

**Kersley**    Then how do you explain the shouting, the quarrelling and the turning over of furniture?

**Sherwood**    I accept Mr Webster's explanation – that there had been another burglary.

**Kersley**    So how did this burglar enter the building, when there was no sign of a break-in?

**Sherwood**    Via the fire escape and the kitchen window.

**Kersley**    But the window had been opened from the inside?

**Sherwood**    My wife often opened it on a warm evening.

**Kersley**    In March? Ah, I see, so it was your wife who let the burglar in?

**Sherwood**    That's a ridiculous suggestion, Mr Kersley, and you know it.

**Kersley**    As ridiculous as suggesting that it was a burglar who caused the bruising on her arm.

**Sherwood**    Not at all. The bruising could have been caused by a struggle with the burglar.

**Kersley**    Rather than a struggle with you?

**Sherwood**    Why should she be struggling with me?

**Kersley**    Because when you returned to inject her, you were horrified to discover she hadn't drunk the glass of wine that contained the sedative you had prepared for her.

**Sherwood**    Then how do you explain the unopened ampoule left in my bag?

**Kersley**    Because you left it there, Mr Sherwood, having only managed to inject five of the ampoules before you were interrupted by Mr Webster, when you fled to the kitchen, dropping the rubber glove on the floor.

**Sherwood**    Have you forgotten that the glove belonged to my wife?

**Kersley**    Have you forgotten that it was soaked in Potassium Chloride?

**Sherwood**    From a bottle of grapefruit juice – as Professor Forsyth confirmed.

**Kersley**    From an injection, that induced a heart attack, as Professor Forsyth demonstrated.

**Sherwood**    The heart attack was probably caused by the intruder.

**Kersley**    Re-enter the intruder, who conveniently appears whenever you're in trouble. No, the truth is that there never was an intruder, Mr Sherwood, because it was you . . .

**Barrington**    My Lord, I must object. My learned friend is putting words into the defendant's mouth.

**Judge**    I agree with you, Sir James. Mr Kersley, you must stop attempting to be the witness as well as prosecuting council. If I were to allow this to continue much longer, you might well end up being the judge as well.

**Kersley**    As Your Lordship pleases.

**Judge** (*furious*)    In future, Mr Kersley, allow the defendant to answer the questions and the jury to decide on the facts.

**Kersley**    Is it a fact, Mr Sherwood, that you kissed Ms Mitchell at the staff Christmas party?

**Sherwood** (*pause*)    Yes – I've already admitted to that.

**Kersley**    And then you left the party a few minutes later?

**Sherwood**    Yes, I did.

**Kersley**   Did Ms Mitchell leave with you?

**Sherwood**   No, she did not.

**Kersley**   Several people were present at that party, Mr Sherwood.

**Sherwood**   I'm not saying she didn't leave at the same time. I'm simply pointing out that she didn't leave with me.

**Kersley**   A nice distinction. But did you then offer to accompany her home?

**Sherwood**   No, we went our separate ways.

**Kersley**   Was it raining at the time?

**Sherwood**   No, it began to rain later.

**Kersley**   Just as you arrived back at her house?

**Sherwood**   I've never been to her flat.

**Kersley**   I didn't say flat, Mr Sherwood, I said house.

**Sherwood**   I've never been to her flat, her appartment or her house. I don't even know where Oldfield Road is.

**Kersley**   Oldfield Road? Who mentioned Oldfield Road?

**Sherwood**   Ms Mitchell must have done when she gave her evidence.

**Kersley**   I don't think so, Mr Sherwood, she referred to Tooting, but she made no mention of Oldfield Road. I could always call for the court transcript, just to be sure.

**Sherwood**   Then I must have seen it written on her file somewhere, but I have no idea where it is.

**Kersley**   Do you know where your office is by any chance, Mr Sherwood?

**Sherwood**   Yes, of course I do.

**Kersley**   And did Ms Mitchell lie when she told the court you asked to see her in your office the following morning?

**Sherwood**    No. I wanted to apologise more formally for what had happened at the staff Christmas party.

**Kersley**    And her response was to unbutton her uniform?

**Sherwood**    Yes, that's exactly what she did.

**Kersley**    Was that before or after you had locked the door?

**Sherwood**    I didn't lock the door.

**Kersley**    So you didn't have sex with her on the couch?

**Sherwood**    Mr Kersley, I'm a surgeon not a film director.

**Kersley**    So it's pure fantasy for her to suggest that you regularly visited her flat in the early hours of the morning?

**Sherwood**    I never visited her flat at any hour of the night or day.

**Kersley**    And you never took her out for dinner or to the theatre?

**Sherwood**    No, I did not.

**Kersley**    Have you seen the play, *The Real Thing*.

**Sherwood** (*pause*)    I may have done.

**Kersley**    And whom did you see it with, Mr Sherwood?

**Sherwood**    I don't recall – probably my wife.

**Kersley**    Yet another person who is conveniently unable to confirm or deny your story. So allow me to try to refresh your memory, because we are now in possession of the two programmes for the plays Ms Mitchell says you took her to see. (*He holds up two programmes.*) *An Inspector Calls*, and *The Real Thing*.

**Sherwood**    That doesn't prove I took Jennifer.

**Kersley**    Jennifer. No it doesn't, but you will recall that Ms Mitchell – I do apologise – Jennifer, was also in the habit of making notes in her diary, and that diary has been in the court's safe keeping for several weeks. I wonder My Lord if you would allow the Usher to pass Ms Mitchell's diary – exhibit four – across to Mr Sherwood.

**Judge**   Yes. Usher. (**Usher** *hands the diary to the defendant.*)

**Kersley**   Please turn to February the fifteenth, 1999 Mr Sherwood, and read to the court Jennifer's entry for that evening.

**Sherwood**   7.30 *The Real Thing.*

**Kersley**   Yes, but do read on, Mr Sherwood. Isn't there another entry below that?

**Sherwood** (*hesitates*)   P.S. at the Albery Theatre.

**Kersley**   P.S. Patrick Sherwood, I suspect – unless, of course, Jennifer had an assignation with Peter Stringfellow.

**Sherwood**   Post script seems more likely, Mr Kersley.

**Kersley**   But she stated unequivocally that it was you.

**Sherwood**   She also stated unequivocally that I drove her home when I don't own a car or even have a driving licence.

**Kersley**   No. No, Mr Sherwood, Ms Mitchell never claimed that you drove her home. Her exact words in reply to your learned counsel were, (*Picks up a sheet of paper.*) 'He always *took* me home' and if you would like her to explain what she meant by that, Mr Sherwood, we can always call her back as she would still be under oath.

**Sherwood**   Why bother, when the oath means nothing to her?

**Kersley**   Are you suggesting that Jennifer committed perjury?

**Sherwood**   Your words, not mine, Mr Kersley.

**Kersley**   But why should she do that?

**Sherwood**   'Mr Sherwood, you will live to regret this.'

**Kersley**   Your words, not hers – because there's no proof she ever said them.

**Sherwood**   Ask any doctor at St George's and they'll tell you about Ms Mitchell's reputation.

**Kersley**   What a gallant fellow you are, Mr Sherwood, which would explain why you dumped her the moment she'd served her purpose.

**Sherwood**   You can't dump someone with whom you've never had a relationship.

**Kersley**   Wouldn't you describe having an affair for three months as a relationship?

**Sherwood**   Yes, I would, but I wouldn't describe one drunken kiss as having an affair.

**Kersley**   But if you weren't having an affair with Jennifer, why would she bother to go to Wellingborough to pick up those drugs for you?

**Sherwood**   She didn't go to Wellingborough to pick up those drugs until after I'd thrown her out of my office.

**Kersley**   Or was it after you'd had 'after-rounds sex' with her in your office?

**Sherwood**   You've crawled back into the gutter, Mr Kersley.

**Kersley**   I'm searching for you, Mr Sherwood.

**Sherwood**   Then you won't find me there.

**Kersley**   But I will find you in your flat pouring your wife a glass of wine. How did you get in? And then adding a sedative. How did you get in? And then leaving without your doctor's bag. How did you get in? And then returning via the fire escape. How did you get in? And then injecting her with five ampoules of Potassium Chloride. How did you get in? And then leaving her to die a slow, painful and terrible death.

**Sherwood**    Nothing could be further from the truth.

**Kersley**    I cannot think of a more accurate summing-up of your entire evidence. No more questions, My Lord.

**Judge**    Sir James, do you wish to re-examine?

**Barrington**    My Lord, it would be a travesty of justice were I not to do so. My learned friend has suggested that if the Jury conclude that Mr Sherwood did have an affair with Ms Mitchell, then they must dismiss the rest of his evidence as a tissue of lies. I now intend to prove beyond reasonable doubt that no such affair ever took place. But to do that I must return to your love of sailing, Mr Sherwood. When the Falklands armada was being assembled, were you called up to join the fleet?

**Sherwood**    Yes, in 1982 I was still on the Reserve list.

**Barrington**    And in what capacity were you asked to serve?

**Sherwood**    As a surgeon captain to the fleet.

**Barrington**    And to which ship were you assigned?

**Sherwood**    HMS *Sheffield*.

**Barrington**    And were you on board that gallant vessel when she was hit by an Exocet and went down in flames?

**Sherwood**    Yes, I was, Sir James, and most fortunate to be among those who survived.

**Barrington**    And while you were in the water, Mr Sherwood, were you burned -- which would account for the small scar on your right forearm, which Ms Mitchell referred to as intimate knowledge only a lover could have been aware of?

**Sherwood**    Yes, Ms Mitchell is quite right about the burn.

**Barrington**    Would you show it to the jury? (**Sherwood** *takes off his jacket and rolls up his sleeve to reveal a small burn.*)

Now, she would have seen that every day in the operating theatre?

**Sherwood**   Yes and whenever I was scrubbing up.

**Barrington**   And whenever you were making love?

**Sherwood**   We never made love.

**Barrington**   Because if you had done so, you would have taken your shirt off?

**Sherwood**   Yes, I would.

**Barrington**   Would you please turn round now Mr Sherwood? Would you please take you shirt off? (*He does so, to reveal a large burn that almost covers his back.*) 'A small burn on his right arm . . . Only when he takes his shirt off!' No more questions My Lord.

*The lights fade as everyone stares at* **Sherwood**'s *back.*


## Scene Two

*The following morning.*
**Jury Bailiff** *walks through the door and once again comes face to face with the audience. The clock shows 9.45 a.m.*

**Jury Bailiff**   Good morning Ladies and Gentlemen of the Jury, on what will be our last day together. When we return to the court in a few moments' time, Mr Justice Cartwright will begin his summing up. He will only give you guidance on points of law. He will not offer an opinion on the case, as that is solely your prerogative. After he has completed his summing up, I will accompany you back here to the jury room, where I will leave you to consider your verdict. (*The* **Jury Bailiff** *glances at the clock, which shows 9.50.*) The time has come for us to make our way back to Court Number One. Ladies and Gentlemen of the Jury, please follow me.

**Jury Bailiff** *steps through the door, so that when the lights come up we are back in Court Number One. Everyone is in place awaiting the* **Judge** *and jury.*

**Usher**    Be upstanding in the court. All persons having anything to do before my Lords, the Queen's Justices, oyer and terminer, and general gaol delivery for the jurisdiction of the Central Criminal Court, draw near and give your attendance. God save the Queen.

*The* **Judge** *enters. When he is in place, they all bow and he returns their bow.*

**Judge**    Ladies and Gentlemen of the Jury. Having heard the arguments from both leading Counsel, it is now your solemn task to return a verdict as to whether Mr Patrick Sherwood be guilty or not guilty of murder.

Among the matters you will have to decide is did Mr Sherwood instruct Ms Mitchell to have six ampoules of Potassium Chloride made up outside London. Or was it compelling evidence – as Sir James suggested – that five out of the six prescriptions were not made out for a Friday – the day on which Ms Mitchell insists Mr Sherwood handed them over to her?

And then you will want to turn your attention to the open window leading to the Sherwoods' fire escape, the rubber glove dropped on the kitchen floor, the wineglass found by Mrs Sherwood's side and the doctor's bag left by the telephone. Are they simply four red herrings, or do they point to something far more sinister? And remember that when it comes to reaching your final decision, you must deal only with facts.

Yes, it is a fact that the rubber glove was found to have a deposit of Potassium on it – but was it concentrated grapefruit juice? Yes, it is a fact that an excess of Temazepam was discovered in Mrs Sherwood's wine – but who put it there? And at the same time, you will want to consider the victim's words, 'How did you get in?'. Were they addressed to the porter, Mr Webster, as he entered the room, or to someone else who quickly disappeared into the kitchen?

Did Mr Sherwood return to the flat that night, in order to inject his wife with Potassium Chloride, or was he, as he claims, signing a death certificate in Westminster? You are in possession of that death certificate which unquestionably bears his signature and is timed at 10.27 p.m., but was it signed that night or later the following morning? Unfortunately, no one has come forward to verify either account, so only you can decide.

Which takes me on to the significance of a life insurance policy for one million pounds, taken out only weeks before Mrs Sherwood suffered her first heart attack. Did you find this a compelling motive for murder, or just another red herring?

Now we come to the most crucial question in this whole case. Did Ms Mitchell – as she vehemently insisted – have an affair with Mr Sherwood that lasted for several months, or are you persuaded that, having been rejected by him, she made the whole story up? Were you affected by the fact that he obviously knew where she lived or were you more struck by seeing the scar on his back? Although you will recall Ms Mitchell told us that whenever they made love Mr Sherwood insisted that the lights were out. You have been able to observe both of them in the witness box, so you can draw your own conclusions as to which one you feel was telling the truth. For certainly, one of them is a brazen liar.

If you decide it was Ms Mitchell who was being deceitful about her relationship with Mr Sherwood, then you have every right to be sceptical about the rest of her evidence. But if, on the other hand, you are convinced she did have an affair with the accused, then you might feel that verifies the rest of her story.

And so the time has now come for you to return to the jury room and consider your verdict. If, when you have completed your deliberations, you feel the Defence have made their case, then it is your duty to return a verdict of Not Guilty. But, if you believe the Prosecution has proved its case beyond reasonable doubt, then it is nothing less than your duty to deliver a verdict of Guilty.

May God guide and assist you in your counsels.

*Lights dim in the court.* **Jury Bailiff** *steps through the jury door, into spot, as house lights go up.*

**Jury Bailiff**    Members of the Jury, the time has come for you to make your decision, but do not do so until I instruct you.

It is your task to decide whether you believe Mr Patrick Sherwood is guilty or not guilty of the murder of Elizabeth Sherwood.

I will leave you for a few moments to talk among yourselves and consider your verdict. (*He leaves the stage for 30 seconds.*)

**Usher**    Silence in Court.

**Jury Bailiff**    Please take the monitor from the back of the seat in front of you, and register your verdict, guilty or not guilty, now.

*Pause while the audience place their vote. This can be done with cards or a show of hands.*

**Jury Bailiff**    Thank you, Ladies and Gentlemen of the Jury. We will now return to the court, in order that your verdict may be known.

**Jury Bailiff** *exits through the jury room doors, which split apart.*

### VERDICT

IF THE AUDIENCE DELIVERS THE VERDICT NOT GUILTY:

**Usher**    Silence in court. Bring up the prisoner.

**Sherwood** *returns to the dock.*

**Judge**    Will the foreman please rise. Mr Foreman, have you reached a verdict?

**Foreman** (*on tape, or from the body of the audience*)    Yes, we have, My Lord.

**Judge**    Do you find the prisoner at the bar, Patrick Hugh Sherwood, guilty or not guilty of the murder of Elizabeth Sherwood?

**Foreman**    Not guilty.

**Judge** (*turns to face the defendant in the dock*)    Patrick Hugh Sherwood, you have been found not guilty of the charges laid before you and I therefore discharge you. You are free to leave the court.

**Sherwood** *comes down from the dock and shakes hands with* **Barrington** *and* **Jarvis**.

**Barrington**    Congratulations.

**Sherwood**    Thank you.

**Jarvis**    Well done.

**Sherwood**    Thank you both. But Sir James, may I ask you a question?

**Barrington**    Yes, of course.

**Sherwood**    Am I right in thinking that when a verdict of not guilty has been reached, there can never be a retrial?

**Barrington**    That is correct. In English law, once a jury has acquitted a defendant he cannot be put on trial again for the same offence.

**Sherwood** (*smiles*)    That's a relief.

**Jarvis**    So tell me, Mr Sherwood, how do you intend to celebrate your great victory?

**Sherwood**    I shall go back to work, Mr Jarvis, just as Sir James predicted I would.

*The attention moves to* **Kersley** *and* **Ashton**, *who are chatting on the other side of the stage.*

**Ashton**    I have a feeling it must have been a close-run thing, so what do you imagine tipped the balance?

**Kersley**   The burn on his back, would be my guess. Pity Ms Mitchell didn't stay to hear his evidence. I would like to have seen her face when the good doctor took off his shirt.

**Ashton**   Perhaps the reality is as Sir James suggests, that having been rejected by Mr Sherwood she was simply seeking revenge.

**Kersley**   I'm not convinced it's quite that simple. There's something about this case that doesn't ring true.

**Ashton**   In what way?

**Kersley** (*they start to leave the stage*)   Well, to start with, why didn't Mitchell return to hear the verdict?

*As they depart the* **Jury Bailiff** *walks quickly back on, as* **Sherwood** *is leaving.*

**Jury Bailiff**   Sir, sir. Can I suggest that you stay put for a few more minutes, as there is rather a large crowd gathering on the pavement outside. And once the corridors have been cleared, we can slip you out the back way.

**Sherwood**   That's most thoughtful of you, Mr Pierce, but I'm quite happy to leave by the front. I've nothing to hide.

**Jury Bailiff**   No, of course you haven't, Mr Sherwood indeed, if I may say so, sir, I never doubted for a moment that you were innocent. By the way, the woman Mitchell is hanging around in the corridor trying to get back in, but I didn't . . .

**Sherwood**   No, that's fine, I'm only too happy to see her.

**Mitchell** *runs on to the stage and the* **Jury Bailiff** *exits.*

**Mitchell**   I booked a table for us at the Caprice. No need to hide in Fulham any longer.

**Sherwood**   You were always that confident of the verdict?

**Mitchell**   Of course. Once the jury had seen that scar on your back they were never going to believe that I had slept with you and to quote Mr Kersley, 'A jury that has doubts will never send a man to gaol for the rest of his life.'

**Sherwood**    You were brilliant in the witness box, in fact, Sir James only got the better of you once.

**Mitchell**    And when was that?

**Sherwood**    When he tricked you into writing your signature on the Usher's notepad, to show that you'd lied when you claimed you were right-handed.

**Mitchell**    But I am right-handed. I worked out exactly what Sir James was up to and realised that the image of me signing that pad with my left hand would remain fixed in the jury's minds.

**Sherwood**    Then why didn't you try on the rubber glove?

**Mitchell**    I did, at the police station, and I just couldn't get it on. Elizabeth must have had very small hands.

**Sherwood**    You thought of everything.

**Mitchell**    Yes, and if only Webster hadn't walked in just before I'd finished injecting her we could have been married a year ago.

**Sherwood**    No, I'm afraid not, Jennifer. You see that was something else Mr Kersley was right about … I never intended to marry you in the first place. (*He turns to walk away as the lights fade.*)

CURTAIN

IF THE AUDIENCE DELIVERS THE VERDICT GUILTY:

**Usher**    Silence in court. Bring up the prisoner.

**Sherwood** *returns to the dock.*

**Judge**    Will the foreman please rise. Mr Foreman, have you reached a verdict?

**Foreman**   Yes, we have, My Lord.

**Judge**   Do you find the prisoner at the bar, Patrick Hugh Sherwood, guilty or not guilty of the murder of Elizabeth Sherwood?

**Foreman**   Guilty.

*The* **Judge** *turns to face the prisoner in the dock.*

**Judge**   Patrick Hugh Sherwood, you stand convicted of murder by a jury of your peers. You undoubtedly poisoned your young wife, taking advantage of your special knowledge and training, and in so doing dishonoured your profession. You murdered Elizabeth Sherwood in order to be rid of her and inherit a million pounds. As the law requires, I sentence you to life imprisonment, with the recommendation that you serve a minimum of seventeen years. You may be curious, Mr Sherwood, to discover why I have recommended this particular sentence. Seventeen years is the period of time that was left on the life insurance policy, the profits of which you had planned to enjoy by spending the rest of your life in the luxury of a penthouse apartment in Chelsea with money to spare. You will instead spend those seventeen years in custody at Her Majesty's pleasure, and may God have mercy on your soul.

**Sherwood**'s *head drops into his hand. The attention moves to* **Barrington** *and* **Jarvis**.

**Barrington**   God help the poor man.

**Jarvis**   What do you imagine tipped the balance? It must have been a close-run thing.

**Barrington**   We'll never know, but it can't have helped that we couldn't explain why he'd left his bag behind, when he went on insisting that he was with a patient in Westminster.

**Jarvis** (*nods*)   I know it's the jury's responsibility to decide the verdict, not ours, but I'm still not sure if the man is guilty.

**Barrington**    Neither am I. (*Watches as* **Mitchell** *enters the courtroom and stares at* **Sherwood**.) But I have a feeling that woman is the one person who knows the answer to your question.

**Guard** *approaches the dock, motions* **Sherwood** *to follow him. They walk halfway across the stage.*

**Ashton**    Well, at least this time you beat the old buzzard.

**Kersley**    Did I? (*Stares at* **Barrington**.) I'm not so sure. There's something about this case that doesn't ring true.

**Ashton**    In what way?

**Kersley**    Nothing I can prove, but I have a feeling we would discover what really took place on the night on March the twenty-first if we could only overhear . . .

**Sherwood** *leaves the witness box and begins to walk across the stage.*

**Guard**    Wait there. (*He goes over to another* **Guard** *who completes the paperwork, as* **Mitchell** *walks up behind* **Sherwood**.)

**Sherwood**    You know I didn't kill Elizabeth.

**Mitchell**    Of course I do, but no one is ever going to believe that when you left my flat to go to Westminster and sign that death certificate it was *me* who went to Arcadia Mansions.

**Sherwood**    How did you get in?

**Mitchell**    Via the fire escape and the kitchen window, and if Webster hadn't interrupted me I would have managed all six ampoules . . . ironic when you think about it. If you'd admitted to having an affair, you would have had the perfect alibi, but then, Patrick, I did warn you, you will live to regret this.

CURTAIN